your affectionate Father—

Thomas Campbell

Declaration and Address

Thomas Campbell

Centennial Edition

Twentieth Thousand

Centennial Bureau
203 Bissell Block
Pittsburgh, Pennsylvania

Printed in the United States of America
ISBN 978-1-60135-800-4

This edition follows the original,
page for page, line for line, letter for
letter. Even the type face dupli-
cates that of a hundred years ago
with remarkable exactness.

1908
RECORD PUBLISHING COMPANY
CORAOPOLIS PA.

Centennial Introduction

Thomas Campbell, the author of this pamphlet, did not come suddenly or unnaturally to the place that must be allowed him in the history of the nineteenth century; nor was it a painless process. He was born in county Down, Ireland, February 1st, 1763, of Scotch ancestry of course. Though his father had renounced Romanism for the Church of England he long forbade his eldest son to become a minister of the Anti-Burgher Seceder Presbyterians. His training included complete courses in Glasgow University and Divinity Hall. After his probation he was nine years minister at Ahorey.

More and more his heart cried out against divisions in the family of God. In 1804 at the Synod in Belfast and in 1805 at the joint meeting in Lurgan he led the movement for uniting the two bodies of Seceders. In 1806 he was sent to the General Synod in Glasgow to plead the same cause. The reunion was effected in 1820.

In 1807 he removed to America and began preaching at once in Western Pennsylvania, then a sparsely settled region of the frontier. It is impossible for those living in these happier times to realize the bitterness of the sectarian strife which he found, or the spiritual destitution, moral decay and infidel arrogance that had grown out of this fresh crucifixion of the Christ.

The vigor, originality, scripturalness and brotherliness of his preaching drew many hearers. New friends constantly vied with the steadfast affection of those who had known him in Ireland. Suddenly, to his amazement, the Presbytery of Chartiers censured him for admitting other Presbyterians than Seceders to a communion service held for scattered families on the Allegheny River above Pittsburgh. On appeal the Synod removed the censure but charged him to beware of further offense. Under persistent persecution he withdrew from the Synod's jurisdiction and continued to preach independently until the events herein set forth.

He brought to the supreme task of his life—the writing of this document—incorruptible faith, unconquerable hope and inexhaustible love; the fulness of learning, the poise of reflection and the ripeness of experience. With entire and unconscious effacement of self he sought the glory of Christ and the happiness of mankind.

In the United States, Canada, England, Australasia, and the various mission fields there are in 1908 a million and a third persons organized into independent churches of Christ pursuant, in the main, to the call of this address. Their missionary offerings last year amounted to over a million dollars. Five thousand preachers are in active service and a thousand young men are in schools and colleges preparing for the ministry. A four years' Centennial Campaign for betterment in all phases of individual, local and general Christian life and service is being waged. It will culminate in a great convention at Pittsburgh in 1909.

Though Barton W. Stone and others had taken the same position earlier, and though a score of years elapsed before the amalgamation of these movements and their separation from former alliances, September 7, 1809, is universally accepted as bearing the same relation to the people now known as Disciples of Christ, Christians or Churches of Christ, that July 4, 1776, holds to the United States of America.

Thomas Campbell not only discovered the necessity and the basis of Christian union but he possessed the spirit of it. In the conviction that he was only a hundred years ahead of his age his message is sent forth anew. May He who is the Truth again add His blessing.

DECLARATION

AND

ADDRESS

OF THE

CHRISTIAN ASSOCIATION

OF

WASHINGTON.

WASHINGTON, (Pa.)

Printed by *BROWN & SAMPLE,*

AT THE OFFICE OF "THE REPORTER."

1809.

AT a meeting held at Buffaloe, August 17, 1809, consisting of persons of different religious denominations; most of them in an unsettled state as to a fixed gospel ministry; it was unanimously agreed, upon the considerations, and for the purposes herein after declared, to form themselves into a religious association, designated as above—which they accordingly did, and appointed twenty-one of their number to meet and confer together; and, with the assistance of Mr. Thomas Campbell, minister of the gospel, to determine upon the proper means to carry into effect the important ends of their association : the result of which conference was the following declaration and address, agreed upon and ordered to be printed at the expence and for the benefit of the society, September 7, 1809.

DECLARATION, &c.

 FROM the series of events which have taken place in the churches for many years past, especially in this western country, as well as from what we know in general of the present state of things in the christian world ; we are persuaded that it is high time for us not only to think, but also to act, for ourselves ; to see with our own eyes, and to take all our measures directly and immediately from the Divine Standard : to this alone we feel ourselves divinely bound to be conformed ; as by this alone we must be judged. We are also persuaded that as no man can be *judged* for his brother, so no man can *judge* for his brother : but that every man must be allowed to judge for himself, as every man must bear his own judgment ;—must give an account of himself to God—We are also of opinion that as the divine word is equally binding upon all so all lie under an equal obligation to be bound by it, and it alone ; and not by any human interpretation of it: and that therefore no man has a right to judge his brother, except in so far as he manifestly violates the express letter of the law. That every such judgment is an express violation of the law of Christ, a daring usurpation of his throne, and a gross intrusion upon the rights and liberties of his subjects. We are therefore of opinion that we should beware of such things ; that we should keep at the utmost distance from every thing of this nature ; and, that knowing the judgment of God against them that commit such things ; we should neither do the same ourselves, nor have pleasure in them that do them. Moreover, being well aware from sad experience, of the heinous nature, and pernicious tendency of religious controversy among christians ; tired and sick of the bitter jarrings and janglings of a party spirit, we would desire to be at rest ; and, were it possible, we would also desire to adopt and recommend such measures as would give rest to our brethren throughout all the churches ;— as would restore unity, peace, and purity, to the whole church of God. This desirable rest, however, we utterly despair either to find for ourselves, or to be able to recommend to our brethren, by continuing amidst the diversity and rancour of party contentions, the veering uncertainty and clashings of human opinions : nor indeed, can we reasonably expect to find it any where, but in Christ and his simple word ; which is the same yesterday, and to-day, and forever. Our desire, therefore, for ourselves and our brethren would be, that rejecting human opinions and the inventions of men, as of any authority, or as having any place in the church of God, we might forever cease from farther contentions about such things ; returning to, and holding fast by the original standard ; taking the divine word alone for our rule ; The Holy Spirit for our teacher and guide, to lead us into all truth ; and Christ alone as exhibited in the word, for our salvation that, by so doing, we may be at peace among ourselves, follow peace with all men, and holiness, without which no man shall see the Lord.— Impressed with these sentiments, we have resolved as follows :

I. That we form ourselves into a religious association under the denomination of the Christian Association of Washington—for the sole purpose of promoting simple evangelical christianity, free from all mixture of human opinions and inventions of men.

II. That each member, according to ability, cheerfully and liberally subscribe a certain specified sum, to be paid half yearly, for the purpose of raising a fund to support a pure Gospel Ministry, that shall reduce to practice that whole form of doctrine, worship, discipline, and government, expressly revealed and enjoined in the word of God. And also for supplying the poor with the Holy Scriptures.

III. That this society consider it a duty, and shall use all proper means in its power, to encourage the formation of similar associations; and shall for this purpose hold itself in readiness, upon application, to correspond with, and render all possible assistance to, such as may desire to associate for the same desirable and important purposes.

IV. That this society, by no means considers itself a church, nor does at all assume to itself the powers peculiar to such a society; nor do the members, as such, consider themselves as standing connected in that relation; nor as at all associated for the peculiar purposes of church association;—but merely as voluntary advocates for church reformation; and, as possessing the powers common to all individuals, who may please to associate in a peaceable and orderly manner, for any lawful purpose: namely, the diposal of their time, counsel and property, as they may see cause.

V. That this society, formed for the sole purpose of promoting simple evangelical christianity, shall, to the utmost of its power, countenance and support such ministers, and such only, as exhibit a manifest conformity to the original standard in conversation and doctrine, in zeal and diligence;—only such as reduce to practice that simple original form of christianity, expressly exhibited upon the sacred page; without attempting to inculcate anything of human authority, ot private opinion, or inventions of men, as having any place in the constitution, faith, or worship, of the christian church—or, any thing, as matter of christian faith, or duty, for which there can not be expressly produced a thus saith the Lord either in express terms, or by approved precedent.

VI. That a standing committee of twenty-one members of unexceptionable moral character, inclusive of the sectetary and treasurer, be chosen annually to superintend the interests, and transact the business, of the society. And that said committee be invested with full powers to act and do, in the name and behalf of their constituents, whatever the society had previously determined, for the purpose of carrying into effect the entire object of its institution—and that in case of any emergency, unprovided for in the existing determinations of the society, said committee be empowered to call a *pro re nota* meeting for that purpose.

VII.   That this society meet at least twice a year, viz. On the first Thursday of May and of November, and that the collectors appointed to receive the half-yearly quotas of the promised subscriptions, be in readiness, at or before each meeting, to make their returns to the treasurer, that he may be able to report upon the state of the funds. The next meeting to be held at Washington on the first Thursday of November next.

VIII.   That each meeting of the society be opened with a sermon, the constitution and address read, and a collection lifted for the benefit of the society—and that all communications of a public nature be laid before the society at its half-yearly meetings.

IX.   That this society, relying upon the all-sufficiency of the Church's Head ; and, through His grace, looking with an eye of confidence to the generous liberality of the sincere friends of genuine christianity ; holds itself engaged to afford a competent support to such ministers, as the Lord may graciously dispose to assist, at the request, and by invitation, of the society, in promoting a pure evangelical reformation, by the simple preaching of the everlasting gospel, and the administration of its ordinances in an exact conformity to the Divine Standard as aforesaid—and, that therefore, whatever the friends of the institution shall please to contribute toward the support of ministers in connexion with this society who may be sent forth to preach at considerable distances, the same shall be gratefully received and acknowledged as a donation to its funds.

ADDRESS, &c.

To all that love our Lord Jesus Christ, in sincerity, throughout all the Churches, the following Address is most respectfully submitted.

DEARLY BELOVED BRETHREN,

THAT it is the grand design and native tendency, of our holy religion, to reconcile and unite man to God, and to each other, in truth and love, to the glory of God, and their own present and eternal good, will not, we presume, be denied, by any of the genuine subjects of christianity. The nativity of its Divine Author was announced from heaven, by an host of angels, with high acclamations of "glory to God in the highest, and, on earth, peace and good will toward men." The whole tenor of that divine book which contains its institutes, in all its gracious declarations, precepts, ordinances, and holy examples, most expressly and powerfully inculcates this. In so far, then, as this holy unity and unanimity in faith and love is attained ; just in the same degree, is the glory of God, and the happiness of man, promoted and secured. Impressed with those sentiments, and at the same time greviously affected with those sad divisions which have so awfully interfered with the benign and gracious intention of our holy religion, by exciting its professed subjects to bite and devour one another ; we cannot suppose ourselves justifiable, in withholding the mite of our sincere and humble endeavours, to heal and remove them.

What awful and distressing effects have those sad divisions produced! what adversions, what reproaches, what backbitings, what evil surmisings, what angry contentions, what enmities, what excommunications, and even persecutions! ! ! And indeed, this must in some measure, continue to be the case so long as those schisms exist, for, said the Apostle, where envying and strife is, *there* is confusion and every evil work. What dreary effects of these accursed divisions are to be seen, even in this highly favored country, where the sword of the civil magistrate has not as yet learned to serve at the altar. Have we not seen congregations broken to pieces, neighborhoods of professing christians first thrown into confusion by party contentions, and, in the end, entirely deprived of gospel ordinances ; while in the meantime, large settlements, and tracts of country, remain to this day entirely destitute of a gospel ministry ; many of them in little better than a state of heathenism : the churches being either so weakened with divisions, that they cannot send them ministers ; or, the people so divided among themselves, that they will not receive them. Severals at the same time who live at the door of a preached gospel, dare not in conscience go to hear it, and, of course, enjoy little more advantage in that respect, than if living in the midst of heathens— How seldom do many in those circumstances enjoy the dispensation of the Lord's Supper, that great ordinance of unity and love. How sadly, also, does this broken and confused state of things interfere with that spiritual intercourse amongst christians, one with another, which is so essential to their edification and comfort, in the midst of a present evil world ;—so divided in sentiment, and, of course, living at such distances, that but few of the same opinion or party, can conveniently and frequently assemble for religious purposes ; or enjoy a due frequency of ministerial attentions. And even where things are in a better state with respect to settled churches, how is the tone of discipline relaxed under the influence of a party spirit ; many being afraid to exercise it with due strictness, lest their people should leave them, and under the cloak of some spurious pretence, find refuge in the bosom of another party ; while, lamentable to be told, so corrupt is the church, with those accursed divisions, that there are but few so base, as not to find admission into some professing party or other. Thus, in a great measure, is that scriptural purity of communion banished from the church of God ; upon the due preservation of which, much of her comfort, glory, and usefulness depends. To complete the dread result of our woeful divisions, one evil yet remains, of a very awful nature : the divine displeasure justly provoked with this sad perversion of the gospel of peace, the Lord withholds his gracious influential presence from his ordinances ; and not unfrequently gives up the contentious authors and abettors of religious discord to fall into grievous scandals ; or visits them with judgments, as he did the house of Eli. Thus while professing christians bite and devour one another they are consumed one of another, or fall a prey to the righteous judgment of God : Meantime the truly religious of all parties are grieved, the weak stumbled, the graceless and profane hardened, the mouths of infidels opened to blaspheme religion ; and thus the only thing under heaven, divinely efficacious to promote and secure the present spiritual and eternal good of man even the gospel of the blessed Jesus, is reduced to contempt ; while multitudes deprived of the gospel ministry, as has been observed, fall an easy pray to seducers, and so become the dupes of almost unheard of delusions. Are not such the visible effects of our sad divisions, even in this otherwise happy country—Say, dear brethren, are not these things so ? Is it not then your incumbent duty to endeavour, by all scriptural means, to have those evils remedied? Who will say, that it is not? And does it not peculiarly belong to *you*, who occupy the place of gospel ministers, to be leaders in this laudable undertaking. Much depends upon *your* hearty concurrence and zealous endeavours. The favorable opportunity which Divine Providence has put into your hands, in this happy country, for the accomplishment of so great a good, is in itself, a consideration of no small encouragement. A country happily exempted from the baneful influence of a civil establishment of any peculiar form of christianity—from under the direct influence of the anti-christian hierarchy—and at the same time, from any formal connexion with the devoted nations, that have given their strength and power unto the beast ; in which, of course, no adequate reformation can be accomplished, until the word of God is fulfilled, and the vials of his wrath poured out upon them. Happy exemption, indeed, from being the object of such awful judgments. Still more happy will it be for us, if we duly esteem and improve those great advantages, for the high and valuable ends, for which they are manifestly given ; —and sure where much is given, much also will be required. Can the Lord expect, or require, any thing less, from a people in such unhampered circumstances—from a people so liberally furnished with all means and mercies, than a thorough reformation, in all things civil and religious, according to his word? Why should we suppose it? And would not such an improvement of our precious privileges, be equally conducive to the glory of God, and our own present and everlasting good? The auspicious phenomena of the times, furnish collateral arguments of a very encouraging nature, that our dutiful and pious endeavours shall not be in vain in the Lord. Is it not the day of the Lord's vengeance upon the anti-christian world ; the year of recompences for the controversy of Zion? Surely then the time to favor her is come ; even the set time. And is it not said that Zion shall be built in troublous times? Have not greater efforts been made, and more done, for the pro-mulgation of the gospel among the nations, since the commence-ment of the French revolution than had been for many centuries, prior to that event? And have not the churches both in Europe and America, since that period, discovered a more than usual concern for the removal of contentions, for the healing of divisions, for the restoration of a christian and brotherly intercourse one with another, and for the promotion of each others spiritual good ; as the printed documents, upon those subjects, amply testify? Should *we* not, then, be excited, by these considerations, to concur with all our might, to help forward this good work ; that what yet remains to be done, may be fully accomplished. And what! Tho' the well meant endeavours after union, have not, in some instances, entirely succeeded to this wish of all parties, should this dissuade us from the attempt. Indeed, should christians cease to contend earnestly for the sacred articles of faith and duty once delivered to the saints, on account of the opposition, and scanty success, which, in many instances attend their faithful and honest endeavours ; the divine cause of truth and righteousness might have, long ago, been relin-quished. And is there any thing more formidable in the Goliah schism, than in many other evils which christians have to combat? Or, has the Captain of Salvation sounded a desist from pursuing, or proclaimed a truce with, this deadly enemy, that is sheathing it's sword in the very bowels of his church, rending and mangling his mystical body into pieces. Has he said to his servants, let it alone? If not, where is the warrant for a cessation of endeavours to have it removed? On the other hand, are we not the better instructed by sage experience, how to proceed in this business; having before our eyes the inadvertencies, and mistakes of others, which have hitherto, in many instances, prevented the desired success? Thus taught by experience, and happily furnished with the accumulated instructions of those that have gone before us; earnestly labouring in this good cause; let us take unto ourselves the whole armour of God; and, having our feet shod with the preparation of the gospel of peace, let us stand fast by this important duty, with all perseverance. Let none that love the peace of Zion be discouraged, much less offended, because that an object of such magnitude does not in the first instance, come forth recommended by the express suffrage of the mighty or the many. This consideration, if duly weighed, will neither give offence, nor yield discouragement, to any, that considers the nature of the thing in question, in connexion with what has been already suggested. Is it not a matter of universal right, a duty equally belonging to every citizen of Zion, to seek her good. In this respect, no one can claim a preference above his fellows, as to any peculiar, much less exclusive obligation. And, as for authority, it can have no place in this business; for surely none can suppose themselves invested with a divine right, as to any thing peculiarly belonging to them, to call the attention of their brethren to this dutiful and important undertaking. For our part, we entertain no such arrogant presumption; nor are we inclined to impute the thought to any of our brethren, that this good work should be let alone, till such time as they may think proper to come forward, and sanction the attempt, by their invitation and example. It is an open field, an extensive work, to which all are equally welcome, equally invited.

Should we speak of competency, viewing the greatness of the object, and the manifold difficulties which lie in the way of its accomplishment; we would readily exclaim, with the Apostle, who is sufficient for these things!—But, upon recollecting ourselves, neither would *we* be discouraged; persuaded with him, that, as the work in which we are engaged, so likewise, *our* sufficiency, is of God. But after all, both the mighty and the many are with us. The Lord himself, and all that are truly his people, are declaredly on our side. The prayers of all the churches; nay, the prayers of Christ himself, John 17, 20, 23, and of all that have ascended to his heavenly kingdom, are with us. The blessing out of Zion is pronounced upon our undertaking. Pray for the peace of Jerusalem, they shall prosper that love thee. With such encouragements as these, what should deter us from the heavenly enterprize; or render hopeless the attempt, of accomplishing, in due time, an entire union of all the churches in faith and practice, according to the word of God. Not that we judge ourselves competent to effect such a thing; we utterly disclaim the thought: But we judge it our bounden duty to make the attempt.

B

by using all due means in our power to promote it ; and also that we have sufficient reason to rest assured that our humble and well-meant endeavours, shall not be in vain in the Lord.

The cause that we advocate is not our own peculiar, nor the cause of any party, considered as such ; it is a common cause, the cause of Christ and our brethren of all denominations. All that we presume, then, is to do, what we humbly conceive to be *our* duty, in connexion with our brethren ; to each of whom it equally belongs, as to us, to exert themselves for this blessed purpose. And as we have no just reason to doubt the concurrence of our brethren, to accomplish an object so desirable in itself, and fraught with such happy consequences, so neither can we look forward to that happy event, which will forever put an end to our hapless divisions, and restore to the church its primitive unity, purity and prosperity ; but, in the pleasing prospect of their hearty and dutiful concurrence.

Dearly beloved brethren, why should *we* deem it a thing incredible that the church of Christ, in this highly favored country, should resume that original unity, peace and purity, which belongs to its constitution, and constitutes its glory? Or, is there any thing that can be justly deemed necessary for this desirable purpose, but to conform to the model, and adopt the practice of the primitive church, expressly exhibited in the New Testament. Whatever alterations this might produce in any or all of the churches, should, we think, neither be deemed inadmissible nor ineligible. Surely such alteration would be every way for the better, and not for the worse ; unless we should suppose the divinely inspired rule to be faulty, or defective. Were we, then, in our church constitution and managements, to exhibit a complete conformity to the Apostolick church, would we not be in that respect, as perfect as Christ intended we should be? And should not this suffice us?

It is, to us, a pleasing consideration that all the churches of Christ, which mutually acknowledge each other as such, are not only agreed in the great doctrines of faith and holiness ; but are also materially agreed, as to the positive ordinances of Gospel institution ; so that our differences, at most, are about the things in which the kingdom of God does not consist, that is, about matters of private opinion, or human invention. What a pity, that the kingdom of God should be divided about such things! ! Who then, would not be the first amongst us, to give up with human inventions in the worship of God ; and to cease from imposing his private opinions upon his brethren : that our breaches might *thus* be healed? Who would not willingly conform to the original pattern laid down in the New Testament, for *this* happy purpose? Our dear brethren, of all denominations, will please to consider, that we have our educational prejudices, and particular customs to struggle with as well as they. But this we do sincerely declare, that there is nothing we have hitherto received as matter of faith or practice, which is not expressly taught and enjoined in the word of God, either in express terms, or approved precedent, that we would not heartily relinquish, that so we might return to the origi-

nal constitutional unity of the christian church; and in this happy
unity, enjoy full communion with all our brethren, in peace and
charity. The like dutiful condescension we candidly expect of all
that are seriously impressed with a sense of the duty they owe to
God, to each other, and to their perishing fellow-brethren of mankind. To this we call, we invite, our brethren, of all denominations, by all the sacred motives which we have avouched as the
impulsive reasons of our thus addressing them.

You are all, dear brethren, equally included as the object of our
love and esteem. With you all we desire to unite in the bonds of
an entire christian unity—Christ alone being the head, the centre,
his word the rule—an explicit belief of, and manifest comformity
to it, in all things—*the terms.* More than this, you will not require of us; and less we cannot require of you; nor, indeed, can
we reasonably suppose, any would desire it; for what good purpose
would it serve? We dare neither assume, nor purpose, the trite
indefinite distinction between essentials, and non-essentials, in
matters of revealed truth and duty; firmly persuaded, that, whatever may be their comparative importance, simply considered, the
high obligation of the Divine Authority revealing, or enjoining
them, renders the belief, or performance of them, absolutely essential to us, in so far as we know them. And to be ignorant of
any thing God has revealed, can neither be our duty, nor our pri-
vilege. We humbly presume then, dear brethren, you can have
no relevant objection to meet us upon this ground. And, we again
beseech you, let it be none, that it is the invitation but of a few;
by your accession we shall be many; and whether few, or many,
in the first instance, it is all one with respect to the event,
which must ultimately await the full information, and hearty
concurrence, of all. Besides, whatever is to be done, must
begin—sometime—somewhere; and no matter where, nor by
whom, if the Lord puts his hand to the work, it must surely prosper. And has he not been graciously pleased, upon many signal
occasions, to bring to pass the greatest events from very small
beginnings, and even by means the most unlikely. Duty then is
ours; but events belong to God.

We hope, then, what we urge, will neither be deemed an un-
reasonable nor an unseasonable undertaking. Why should it be
thought unseasonable? Can any time be assigned, while things continue as they are, that would prove more favorable for such an
attempt, or what could be supposed to make it so? Might it be the
approximation of parties to a greater nearness, in point of public
profession and similarity of customs? Or might it be expected from
a gradual decline of bigotry? As to the former, it is a well known
fact, that where the difference is least, the opposition is always
managed with a degree of vehemence, inversely proportioned to
the merits of the cause. With respect to the latter, tho' we are
happy to say, that in some cases and places, and we hope, universally, bigotry is upon the decline: yet we are not warranted, either

by the past or present, to act upon that supposition. We have, as yet, by this means, seen no such effect produced; nor indeed could we reasonably expect it; for there will always be multitudes of weak persons in the church, and these are generally most subject to bigotry; add to this, that while divisions exist, there will always be found interested men, who will not fail to support them :—nor can we at all suppose, that Satan will be idle to improve an advantage, so important to the interests of his kingdom. And, let it be further observed upon the whole; that, in matters of similar importance to our secular interests, we would, by no means content ourselves, with such kind of reasoning. We might further add that the attempt here suggested not being of a partial, but of general nature, it can have no just tendency to excite the jealousy, or hurt the feelings, of any party. On the contrary, every effort towards a permanent scriptural unity amongst the churches, upon the solid basis of universally acknowledged, and self-evident truths, must have the happiest tendency to enlighten and conciliate; by thus manifesting to each other, their mutual charity, and zeal for the truth :—"Whom I loved in the truth, saith the Apostle, and not I only, but also all they that have known the truth; for the truth's sake, which is in us, and shall be with us forever. Indeed if no such divine and adequate basis of union, can be fairly exhibited, as will meet the approbation of every upright and intelligent christian : nor such mode of procedure adopted in favor of the weak, as will not oppress their consciences, then the accomplishment of this grand object upon principle, must be forever impossible.— There would, upon this supposition, remain no other way of accomplishing it, but merely by voluntary compromise, and good natured accommodation. That such a thing however will be accomplished, one way or other, will not be questioned by any that allow themselves to believe, that the commands and prayers of our Lord Jesus Christ will not utterly prove ineffectual. Whatever way, then, it is to be effected; whether upon the solid basis of divinely revealed truth; or the good natured principle of christian forbearance and gracious condescension; is it not equally practicable, equally eligible to us, as ever it can be to any; unless we should suppose ourselves destitute of that christian temper and discernment, which is essentially necessary to qualify us to do the will of our gracious Redeemer, whose expressed command to his people is that there be no division among them; but that they all walk by the same rule, speak the same thing, and be perfectly joined together in the same mind, and in the same judgment? We believe then it is as practicable, as it is eligible. Let us attempt it. "Up and be doing, and the Lord will be with you."

Are we not all praying for that happy event, when there shall be but one fold, as there is but one chief shepherd. What! shall we pray for a thing, and not strive to obtain it! ! not use the necessary means to have it accomplished! ! What said the Lord to Moses upon a piece of conduct somewhat similar? "Why criest thou unto me? Speak unto the children of Israel that they go forward, but lift thou up thy rod, and stretch out thine hand.'' Let the ministers of Jesus but embrace this exhortation, put their hand to the work and encourage the people to go forward upon the firm ground of obvious truth, to unite in the bonds of an entire christian unity ; and who will venture to say, that it would not soon be accomplished? ''Cast ye up, cast ye up, prepare the way, take up the stumbling block out of the way of my people,'' saith your God. To you, therefore, it peculiarly belongs, as the professed and acknowledged leaders of the people, to go before them in this good work—to remove human opinions and the inventions of men out of the way ; by carefully separating this chaff, from the pure wheat of primary and authentic revelation ;—casting out that assumed authority, that enacting and decreeing power, by which those things have been imposed and established. To the ministerial department then do we look with anxiety. Ministers of Jesus, we can neither be ignorant of, nor unaffected with the divisions and corruptions of his church. His dying commands, his last and ardent prayers for, the visible unity of his professing people, will not suffer you to be indifferent in this matter. You will not, you cannot, therefore, be silent, upon a subject of such vast importance to his personal glory and the happiness of his people—consistently you cannot ; for silence gives consent. You will rather lift up your voice like a trumpet to expose the heinous nature, and dreadful consequences of those unnatural and anti-christian divisions, which have so rent and ruined the church of God. Thus, in justice to your station and character, honored of the Lord, would we hopefully anticipate your zealous and faithful efforts to heal the breaches of Zion ; that God's dear children might dwell together in unity and love—But if otherwise—* * * * we forebear to utter it. See Mal. 2, 1—10.

Oh! that ministers and people would but consider, that there are no divisions in the grave ; nor in that world which lies beyond it: there our divisions must come to an end! we must all unite there!— Would to God, we could find in our hearts to put an end to our short-lived divisions here ; that so we might leave a blessing behind us ; even a happy and united church. What gratification, what utility, in the meantime, can our divisions afford either to ministers or people? Should they be perpetuated, 'till the day of judgment would they convert one sinner from the error of his ways, or save a soul from death? Have they any tendency to hide the multitude of sins that are so dishonorable to God, and hurtful to his people? Do they not rather irritate and produce them? How innumerable and highly aggravated are the sins they have produced, and are at this day, producing, both amongst professors and profane. We entreat, we beseach you then, dear brethren, by all those considerations, to concur in this blessed and dutiful attempt—What is the work of all, must be done by all. Such was the work of the tabernacle in the wilderness. Such is the work to which you are called ; not by the authority of man ; but by Jesus Christ and God the

Father, who raised him from the dead. By this authority are you called to raise up the tabernacle of David, that is fallen down amongst us ; and to set it up upon its own base. This you cannot do, while you run every man to his own house, and consult only the interest of his own party. Till you associate, consult, and advise together ; and in a friendly and christian manner explore the subject, nothing can be done. We would therefore, with all due deference and submission, call the attention of our brethren to the obvious and important duty of association. Unite with us in the common cause of simple evangelical christianity—In this glorious cause we are ready to unite with you—United we shall prevail. It is the cause of Christ, and of our brethren throughout all the churches, of catholic unity, peace, and purity—a cause that must finally prosper in spite of all opposition. Let us unite to promote it. Come forward then, dear brethren, and help with us. Do not suffer yourselves to be lulled asleep by that syren song of the slothful and reluctant professor, "The time is not yet come—the time is not come—saith he,—the time that the Lord's house should be built." Believe him not—Do ye not discern the signs of the times? "Have not the two witnesses arisen from their state of political death, from under the long proscription of ages? Have they not stood upon their feet, in the presence, and to the consternation and terror of their enemies? Has not their resurrection been accompanied with a great earthquake? Has not the tenth part of the great city been thrown down by it? Has not this event aroused the nations to indignation? Have they not been angry, yea very angry. Therefore, O Lord, is thy wrath come upon them, and the time of the dead that they should be avenged, and that thou shouldest give reward to thy servants, the Prophets, and to them that fear thy name, both small and great ; and that thou shouldest destroy them that have destroyed the earth. Who amongst us has not heard the report of these things—of these lightnings and thunderings, and voices of this tremendous earthquake and great hail ; of these awful convulsions and revolutions that have dashed and are dashing to pieces the nations like a potter's vessel? Yea, have not the remote vibrations of this dreadful shock been felt even by us, whom Providence has graciously placed at so great a distance? What shall we say to these things? Is it time for us to sit still in our corruptions and divisions, when the Lord by his word and providence, is so loudly and expressly calling us to repentance and reformation? "Awake, awake ; put on thy strength, O Zion, put on thy beautiful garments, O Jerusalem the holy city ; for henceforth there shall no more come unto thee the uncircumcised and the unclean. Shake thyself from the dust, O Jerusalem ; arise, loose thyself from the *bands* of thy neck, O captive daughter of Zion"— Resume that precious, that dear bought liberty, wherewith Christ has made his people free ; a liberty from subjection to any authority but his own, in matters of religion. Call no man father, no man master upon earth ;—for one is your master, even Christ, and all ye are brethren. Stand fast therefore in this precious liberty, and be not entangled again with the yoke of bondage. For the vindication of this precious liberty have we declared ourselves hearty and willing advocates. For this benign and dutiful purpose have we associated, that by so doing, we might contribute the mite of our humble endeavours to promote it, and thus invite our brethren to do the same. As the first fruits of our efforts for this blessed purpose we respectfully present to their consideration the following proposition—relying upon their charity and candour that they will neither despise, nor misconstrue, our humble and adventurous attempt. If they should in any measure serve, as a preliminary, to open up the way to a permanent scriptural unity amongst the friends and lovers of truth and peace throughout the churches, we shall greatly rejoice at it. We by no means pretend to dictate : and could we propose any thing more evident, consistent, and adequate, it should be at their service. Their pious and dutiful attention to an object of such magnitude will induce them to communicate to us their emendations ; and thus what is sown in weakness, will be raised up in power—for certainly the collective graces that are conferred upon the church, if duly united and brought to bear upon any point of commanded duty, would be amply sufficient for the right and successful performance of it. For to one is given by the spirit the word of wisdom ; to another the word of knowledge by the same spirit ; to another faith by the same spirit ; to another the discerning of spirits : but the manifestation of the spirit is given to every man to profit withal. As every man, therefore, hath received the gift, even so minister the same one to another as good stewards of the manifold grace of God. In the face then of such instructions, and with such assurances of an all-sufficiency of divine grace, as the church has received from her exalted Head, we can neither justly doubt the concurrence of her genuine members ; nor yet their ability, when dutifully acting together, to accomplish any thing that is necessary for his glory, and their own good ; and certainly their visible unity in truth and holiness, in faith and love, is, of all things, the most conducive to both these, if we may credit the dying commands and prayers of our gracious Lord. In a matter, therefore, of such confessed importance, our christian brethren, however unhappily distinguished by party names, will not, cannot, withhold their helping hand. We are as heartily willing to be their debtors, as they are indispensably bound to be our benefactors. Come, then, dear brethren, we most humbly beseech you, cause your light to shine upon our weak beginnings, that we may see to work by it. Evince your zeal for the glory of Christ, and the spiritual welfare of your fellow-christians, by your hearty and zealous co-operation to promote the unity, purity and prosperity of his church.

Let none imagine that the subjoined propositions are at all intended as an overture towards a new creed, or standard, for the church, or, as in any wise designed to be made a term of communion ;—nothing can be farther from our intention. They are merely designed for opening up the way, that we may come fairly and firmly to original grounds upon clear and certain premises : and take up things just as the Apostles left them.—That thus disentangled from the accruing embarrassments of intervening ages, we may stand with evidence upon the same ground on which the church stood at the beginning—Having said so much to solicit attention and prevent mistake, we submit as follows:

PROP. 1. THAT the church of Christ upon earth is essentially, intentionally, and constitutionally one ; consisting of all those in every place that profess their faith in Christ and obedience to him in all things according to the scriptures, and that manifest the same by their tempers and conduct, and of none else as none else can be truly and properly called christians.

2. That although the church of Christ upon earth must necessarily exist in particular and distinct societies, locally separate one from another ; yet there ought to be no schisms, no uncharitable divisions among them. They ought to receive each other as Christ Jesus hath also received them to the glory of God. And for this purpose, they ought all to walk by the same rule, to mind and speak the same thing ; and to be perfectly joined together in the same mind, and the same judgment.

3, That in order to this, nothing ought to be inculcated upon christians as articles of faith ; nor required of them as terms of communion ; but what is expressly taught and enjoined upon them, in the word of God. Nor ought any thing be admitted, as of divine obligation, in their church constitution and managements, but what is expressly enjoined by the authority of our Lord Jesus Christ and his Apostles upon the New Testament church ; either in expressed terms, or by approved precedent.

4. That although the scriptures of the Old and New Testament are inseparably connected, making together but one perfect and entire revelation of the Divine will, for the edification and salvation of the church ; and therefore in that respect cannot be separated ; yet as to what directly and properly belongs to their immediate object, the New Testament is as perfect a constitution for the worship, discipline and government of the New Testament church, and as perfect a rule for the particular duties of its members ; as the Old Testament was for the worship discipline and government of the Old Testament church, and the particular duties of its members.

5. That with respect to the commands and ordinances of our Lord Jesus Christ, where the scriptures are silent, as to the express time or manner of performance, if any such there be ; no human authority has power to interfere, in order to supply the supposed deficiency, by making laws for the church ; nor can any thing more be required of christians in such cases, but only that they *so* observe these commands and ordinances, as will evidently answer the declared and obvious end of their institution. Much less has any hu-

man authority power to impose new commands or ordinances upon the church, which our Lord Jesus Christ has not enjoined. Nothing ought to be received into the faith or worship of the church ; or be made a term of communion amongst christians, that is not as old as the New Testament.

6. That although inferences and deductions from scripture premises, when fairly inferred, may be truly called the doctrine of God's holy word : yet are they not formally binding upon the consciences of christians farther than they perceive the connection, and evidently see that they are so ; for their faith must not stand in the wisdom of men ; but in the power and veracity of God—therefore no such deduction can be made terms of communion, but do properly belong to the after and progressive edification of the church. Hence it is evident that no such deductions or inferential truths ought to have any place in the churchs's confession.

7. That although doctrinal exhibitions of the great system of divine truths, and defensive testimonies in opposition to prevailing errors, be highly expedient ; and the more full and explicit they be, for those purposes, the better ; yet as these must be in a great measure the effect of human reasoning, and of course must contain many inferential truths, they ought not to be made terms of christian communion : unless we suppose, what is contrary to fact, that none have a right to the communion of the church, but such as possess a very clear and decisive judgment ; or are come to a very high degree of doctrinal information ; whereas the church from the beginning did, and ever will, consist of little children and young men, as well as fathers.

8. That as it is not necessary that persons should have a particular knowledge or distinct apprehension of all divinely revealed truths in order to entitle them to a place in the church ; neither should they, for this purpose, be required to make a profession more extensive than their knowledge : but that on the contrary their having a due measure of scriptural self-knowledge respecting their lost and perishing condition by nature and practice ; and of the way of salvation thro' Jesus Christ, accompanied with a profession of their faith in, and obedience to him, in all things according to his word, is all that is absolutely necessary to qualify them for admission into his church.

9. That all that are enabled, thro' grace, to make such a profession, and to manifest the reality of it in their tempers and conduct, should consider each other as the precious saints of God, should love each other as brethren, children of the same family and father, temples of the same spirit, members of the same body, subjects of the same grace, objects of the same divine love, bought with the same price, and joint heirs of the same inheritance. Whom God hath thus joined together no man should dare to put asunder.

10. That division among christians is a horrid evil, fraught with many evils. It is anti-christian, as it destroys the visible unity of the body of Christ ; as if he were divided against himself, exclu-

ding and excommunicating a part of himself. It is anti-scriptural, as being strictly prohibited by his sovereign authority; a direct violation of his express command. It is anti-natural, as it excites christians to contemn, to hate and oppose one another, who are bound by the highest and most endearing obligations to love each other as brethren, even as Christ has loved them. In a word, it is productive of confusion, and of every evil work.

11. That, (in some instances,) a partial neglect of the expressly revealed will of God; and, (in others,) an assumed authority for making the approbation of human opinions, and human inventions, a term of communion by introducing them into the constitution, faith, or worship, of the church: are, and have been, the immediate, obvious, and universally acknowledged causes, of all the corruptions and divisions that ever have taken place in the church of God.

12. That all that is necessary to the highest state of perfection and purity of the church upon earth is, first, that none be received as members, but such as having that due measure of scriptural self-knowledge described above, do profess their faith in Christ and obedience to him in all things according to the scriptures; nor, 2dly, that any be retained in her communion longer than they continue to manifest the reality of their profession by their tempers and conduct. 3dly, that her ministers, duly and scripturally qualified, inculcate none other things than those very articles of faith and holiness expressly revealed and enjoined in the word of God. Lastly, that in all their administration they keep close by the observance of all divine ordinances, after the example of the primitive church, exhibited in the New Testament; without any additions whatsoever of human opinions or inventions of men.

13. Lastly. That if any circumstantial indispensably necessary to the observance of divine ordinances be not found upon the page of express revelation, such, and such only, as are absolutely necessary for this purpose, should be adopted, under the title of human expedients, without any pretence to a more sacred origin —so that any subsequent alteration or difference in the observance of these things might produce no contention nor division in the church.

From the nature and construction of these propositions, it will evidently appear, that they are laid in a designed subserviency to the declared end of our association; and are exhibited for the express purpose of performing a duty of previous necessity—a duty loudly called for in existing circumstances at the hands of every one, that would desire to promote the interests of Zion—a duty not only enjoined, as has been already observed from Is. 57, 14, but which is also there predicted of the faithful remnant as a thing in which they would voluntarily engage. "He that putteth his trust in me shall possess the land, and shall inherit my holy mountain; and shall say, cast ye up, cast ye up, prepare the way; take up the stumbling block out of the way of my people." To prepare the way for a permanent scriptural unity amongst christians, by calling up to their consideration fundamental truths, directing their attention to first principles, clearing the way before them by removing the stumbling blocks—the rubbish of ages which has been thrown upon it, and fencing it on each side, that in advancing towards the desired object, they may not miss the way through mistake, or inadvertency, by turning aside to the right hand or to the left—is, at least, the sincere intention of the above propositions. It remains with our brethren, now to say, how far they go toward answering this intention. Do they exhibit truths demonstrably evident in the light of scripture and right reason; so that to deny any part of them the contrary assertion would be manifestly absurd and inadmissible? Considered as a preliminary for the above purpose, are they adequate; so that if acted upon, they would infallibly lead to the desired issue—If evidently defective in either of these respects, let them be corrected and amended, till they become sufficiently evident, adequate, and unexceptionable. In the mean time let them be examined with rigor, with all the rigor that justice, candour, and charity will admit. If we have mistaken the way, we shall be glad to be set right ;—but if, in the mean time, we have been happily led to suggest obvious and undeniable truths, which if adopted and acted upon, would infallibly lead to the desired unity, and secure it when obtained ; we hope it will be no objection, that they have not proceeded from a general council. It is not the voice of the multitude, but the voice of truth, that has power with the conscience—that can produce rational conviction, and acceptable obedience. A conscience that awaits the decision of the multitude, that hangs in suspence for the casting vote of the majority, is a fit subject for the man of sin. This we are persuaded is the uniform sentiment of real christians of every denomination. Would to God that all professors were such—then should our eyes soon behold the prosperity of Zion ; we should soon see Jerusalem a quiet habitation. Union in truth has been, and ever must be, the desire and prayer of all such—Union in Truth is our motto. The Divine Word is our Standard ; in the Lord's name do we display our banners. Our eyes are upon the promises; "So shall they fear the name of the Lord from the west, and his glory from the rising of the sun." When the enemy shall come in like a flood the spirit of the Lord shall lift up a standard against him." Our humble desire is to be his standard bearers—to fight under *his* banner, and with *his* weapons, "which are not carnal ; but mighty through God to the pulling down of strong holds ;" even all these strong holds of division, those partition walls of separation ; which, like the wall of Jericho, have been built up, as it were, to the very heavens, to separate God's people, to divide *his* flock and so to prevent them from entering into their promised rest, at least in so far as it respects this world. An enemy hath done this ; but he shall not finally prevail ;—"for the meek shall inherit the earth, and shall delight themselves in the abundance of peace." And the kingdom and dominion, even the greatness of the kingdom under the whole heaven, shall be given to the people of the saints of the Most High, and they shall possess it forever.'' But this cannot be in their present broken and divided state, ''for a kingdom, or an house divided against itself cannot stand, but cometh to desolation.'' Now this has been the case with the church for a long time. However, ''the Lord will not cast off his people, neither will he forsake his heritage, but judgment shall return unto righteousness, and all the upright in heart shall follow it.'' To all such, and such alone, are our expectations directed. Come, then, ye blessed of the Lord, we have your prayers, let us also have your actual assistance. What, shall we pray for a thing and not strive to obtain it!

We call, we invite you again, by every consideration in these premises. You that are near, associate with us; you that are at too great a distance, associate as we have done—Let not the paucity of your number in any given district, prove an insuperable discouragement. Remember him that has said, ''if two of you shall agree on earth as touching any thing that they shall ask, it shall be done for them of my father which is in heaven: for where two or three are gathered together in my name, there am I in the midst of them.'' With such a promise as this for the attainment of every possible and promised good, there is no room for discouragement. Come on, then, ''ye that fear the Lord keep not silence, and give him no rest till he make Jerusalem a joy and a praise in the earth. Put on that noble resolution dictated by the prophet, saying, ''for Zion's sake will we not hold our peace, and for Jerusalem's sake we will not rest until the righteousness thereof go forth as brightness, and the salvation thereof as a lamp that burneth.''— Thus impressed, ye will find means to associate at such convenient distances, as to meet, at least, once a month, to beseech the Lord to put an end to our lamentable divisions; to heal and unite his people, that his church may resume her original constitutional unity and purity, and thus be exalted to the enjoyment of her promised prosperity—that the Jews may be speedily converted, and the fullness of the Gentiles brought in. Thus associated, you will be in a capacity to investigate the evil causes of our sad divisions; to consider and bewail their pernicious effects; and to mourn over them before the Lord—who hath said, ''I will go and return to my place, till they acknowledge their offence and seek my face.'' Alas! then, what reasonable prospect can we have of being delivered from those sad calamities, which have so long afflicted the church of God; while a party spirit, instead of bewailing, is every where justifying, the bitter principle of these pernicious evils; by insisting upon the right of rejecting those, however unexceptionable in other respects, who cannot see with them in matters of private opinion, of human inference, that are no where expressly revealed or enjoined in the word of God.—Thus associated, will the friends of peace, the advocates for christian unity, be in a capacity to connect in large circles, where several of those smaller societies may meet semi-annually at a convenient centre, and thus avail themselves of their combined exertions for promoting the interests ot the common cause. We hope that many of the Lord's ministers in all places will volunteer in this service, forasmuch as they know, it is his favorite work, the very desire of his soul.

Ye lovers of Jesus, and beloved of him, however scattered in this cloudy and dark day, ye love the truth as it is in Jesus, (if our hearts deceive us not) so do we. Ye desire union in Christ, with all them that love him ; so do we. Ye lament and bewail our sad divisions ; so do we. Ye reject the doctrines and commandments or men that ye may keep the law of Christ ; so do we. Ye believe the alone sufficiency of his word ; so do we. Ye believe that the word itself ought to be our rule and not any human explication of it ; so do we. Ye believe that no man has a right to judge, to exclude, or reject, his professing christian brother ; except in so far as he stands condemned, or rejected, by the express letter of the law :—so do we. Ye believe that the great fundamental law of unity and love ought not to be violated to make way for exalting human opinions to an equality with express revelation, by making them articles of faith and terms of communion—so do we. Ye sincere and impartial followers of Jesus, friends of truth and peace, we dare not, we cannot, think otherwise of you ;—it would be doing violence to your character ; —it would be inconsistent with your prayers and profession, so to do. We shall therefore have *your* hearty concurrence. But if any of our dear brethren, from whom we should expect better things, should through weakness or prejudice, be in any thing otherwise minded, than we have ventured to suppose, we charitably hope, that, in due time, God will reveal even this unto them :—Only let such neither refuse to come to the light ; nor yet through prejudice, reject it, when it shines upon them. Let them rather seriously consider what we have thus most seriously and respectfully submitted to their consideration, weigh every sentiment in the balance of the sanctuary, as in the sight of God, with earnest prayer for, and humble reliance upon his spirit ; and not in the spirit of self-sufficiency and party zeal,—and, in so doing, we rest assured, the consequence will be happy, both for their own, and the church's peace. Let none imagine, that in so saying, we arrogate to ourselves a degree of intelligence superior to our brethren, much less superior to mistake—so far from this, our confidence is entirely founded upon the express scripture and matter of fact evidence, of the things referred to ; which may nevertheless, through inattention, or prejudice, fail to produce their proper effect ;—as has been the case, with respect to some of the most evident truths, in a thousand instances.—But charity thinketh no evil : and we are far from surmising, though we must speak. To warn even against possible evils, is certainly no breach of charity, as to be confident of the certainty of some things, is no just argument of presumption. We by no means claim the approbation of our brethren, as to any thing we have suggested for promoting the sacred cause of christian unity; farther than it carries its own evidence along with it: but we humbly claim a fair investigation of the subject; and solicit the assistance of our brethren for carrying into effect what we have thus weakly attempted. It is our consolation, in the mean time, that the desired event, as certain as it will be happy and glorious, admits of no dispute; however we may hesitate, or differ, about the proper means of promoting it. All we shall venture to say as to this, is that we trust we have taken the proper ground, at least, if we have not, we despair of finding it elsewhere. For if holding fast in profession and practice whatever is expressly revealed and enjoined in the divine standard does not under the promised influence of the divine spirit, prove an adequate basis for promoting and maintaining unity, peace and purity, we utterly despair of attaining those invaluable privileges, by adopting the standard of any party. To advocate the cause of unity while espousing the interests of a party would appear as absurd, as for this country to take part with either of the beligerents in the present awful struggle, which has convulsed and is convulsing the nations, in order to maintain her neutrality and secure her peace. Nay, it would be adopting the very means, by which the bewildered church has, for hundreds of years past, been rending and dividing herself into fractions; for Christ's sake and for the truth's sake; though the first and foundation truth of our christianity is union with him, and the very next to it in order, union with each other in him—"that we receive each other, as Christ has also received us: to the glory of God." For this is his commandment that we believe in his son Jesus Christ, and love one another, as he gave us commandment. And he that keepeth his commandments dwelleth in him, and he in him—and hereby we know that he dwelleth in us, by the spirit which he hath given us"—even the spirit of faith, and of love, and of a sound mind. And surely this should suffice us. But how to love, and receive our brother; as we believe and hope Christ has received both him and us, and yet refuse to hold communion with him, is we confess, a mystery too deep for us. If this be the way that Christ hath received us, then woe is unto us. We do not here intend a professed brother trangressing the expressed letter of the law, and refusing to be reclaimed.— Whatever may be our charity in such a case, we have not sufficient evidence that Christ hath received him, or that he hath received Christ as his teacher and Lord. To adopt means, then, apparently subversive of the very end proposed, means which the experience of ages has evinced successful only in overthrowing the visible interests of christianity; in counteracting, as far as possible, the declared intention, the expressed command of its Divine Author; would appear in no wise a prudent measure for removing and preventing those evils. To maintain unity and purity has always been the plausible pretence of the compilers and abettors of human systems; and we believe in many instances their sincere intention:

but have they at all answered the end? Confessedly, demonstrably, they have not—no, not even in the several parties which have most strictly adopted them—much less to the catholic professing body. Instead of her catholic constitutional unity and purity, what does the church present us with, at this day, but a catalogue of sects and sectarian systems; each binding its respective party by the mose sacred and solemn engagements, to continue as it is to the end of the world; at least this is confessedly the case with many of them. What a sorry substitute these, for christian unity and love. On the other hand, what a mercy is it, that no human obligation that man can come under is valid against the truth. When the Lord the healer, descends upon his people, to give them a discovery of the nature and tendency of those artificial bonds, wherewith they have suffered themselves to be bound, in their dark and sleepy condition: they will no more be able to hold them in a state of sectarian bondage; than the withs and cords with which the Philistines bound Sampson were able to retain him their prisoner; or, than the bonds of anti-christ were, to hold in captivity the fathers of the reformation. May the Lord soon open the eyes of his people to see these things in their true light; and excite them to come up out of their wilderness condition—out of this Babel of confusion—leaning upon their beloved, and embracing each other in him; holding fast the unity of the spirit in the bonds of peace. This gracious unity and unanimity in Jesus would afford the best external evidence of their union with him; and of their conjoint interest in the Father's love. By this shall all men know that ye are my disciples, saith he, if ye have love one to another. And "this is my commandment that ye love one another as I have loved you; that ye also love one another." And again, "Holy Father, keep through thine own name, those whom thou hast given me that they may be one as we are," even "all that shall believe in me—that they all may be one; as thou Father art in me and I in thee, that they also may be one in us; that the world may believe that thou hast sent me. And the glory which thou gavest me; I have given them, that they may be one, even as we are one: I in them and thou in me, that they may be made perfect in me; and that the world may know that thou hast sent me, and hast loved them, as thou hast loved me." May the Lord hasten it in his time. Farewell.

Peace be with all them that love our Lord Jesus Christ in sincerity. Amen.

THOS. CAMPBELL, Secretary.

THOS. ACHESON, Treasurer.

APPENDIX.

TO prevent mistakes we beg leave to subjoin the following explanations. As to what we have done—our reasons for so doing —and the grand object we would desire to see accomplished—all these, we presume, are sufficiently declared in the foregoing pages. As to what we intend to do in our associate capacity, and the ground we have taken in that capacity, tho' expressly and definitely declared ; yet, these, perhaps, might be liable to some misconstruction.— First, then, we beg leave to assure our brethren, that we have no intention to interfere, either directly, or indirectly, with the peace and order of the settled churches, by directing any ministerial assistance, with which the Lord may please to favour us, to make inroads upon such ; or, by endeavouring to erect churches out of churches—to distract and divide congregations. We have no nos- trum, no peculiar discovery of our own to propose to fellow-chris- tians, for the fancied importance of which, they should become followers of us. We propose to patronize nothing but the inculca- tion of the express word of God—either as to matter of faith or practice ;—but every one that has a Bible and can read it, can read this for himself.—Therefore we have nothing new. Neither do we pretend to acknowledge persons to be ministers of Christ, and, at the same time, consider it our duty to forbid, or discourage people to go to hear them, merely because they may hold some things disagreeable to us ; much less to encourage their people to leave them on that account ;—and such do we esteem all, who preach a free unconstitutional salvation through the blood of Jesus to per- ishing sinners of every description ; and who manifestly connect with this a life of holiness, and pastoral diligence in the perform- ance of all the duties of their sacred office according to the scrip- tures ; even all, of whom, as to all appearance, it may be truly said to the object of their charge, "they seek not *yours*, but *you*." May the good Lord prosper all such, by whatever name they are called ; and fast hasten that happy period, when Zion's watchmen shall see eye to eye, and all be called by the same name. *Such* then have nothing to fear from our association, were our resources equal to our utmost wishes. But all others we esteem as hirelings, as idle shepherds; and should be glad to see the Lord's flock de- livered from their mouth, according to his promise. Our princi- pal and proper design, then, with respect to ministerial assistants, such as we have described in our fifth resolution, is to direct their attention to those places where there is manifest need for their labours ; and many such places there are ; would to God it were in our power to supply them. As to creeds and confessions, although we may appear to our brethren to oppose them, yet this is to be understood only in *so far* as they oppose the unity of the church, by containing sentiments not expressly revealed in the word of God; or by the way of using them, become the instruments of a human or implicit faith : or, oppress the weak of God's heritage : where they are liable to none of those objections, we have nothing against them. It is the *abuse* and not the *lawful use* of such compilations that we oppose. See PROP. 7, page 17. Our intention therefore, with respect to all the churches of Christ is perfectly amicable. We heartily wish their reformation ; but by no means their hurt or confusion. Should any affect to say, that our coming forward as we have done, in advancing and publishing such things, have a manifest tendency to distract and divide the churches, or to make a new party ; we treat it as a confident and groundless assertion : and must suppose they have not duly considered, or at least, not well understood the subject.

All we shall say to this at present, is, that if the divine word be not the standard of a party—Then are we not a party, for we have adopted no other. If to maintain its alone sufficiency be not a party principle : then are we not a party—If to justify this principle by our practice, in making a rule of it, and of *it alone ;* and not of our own opinions, nor of those of others be not a party principle—then are we not a party—If to propose and practice neither more nor less than it expressly reveals and enjoins be not a partial business, then are we not a party. These are the very sentiments we have approved and recommended, as a society formed for the express purpose of promoting christian unity, in opposition to a party spirit. Should any tell us that to do these things is impossible without the intervention of human reason and opinion. We humbly thank them for the discovery. But who ever thought otherwise? Were we not rational subjects, and of course capable of understanding and forming opinions ; would it not evidently appear, that, to us, revelation of any kind would be quite useless ; even suppose it as evident as mathematicks. We pretend not, therefore, to divest ourselves of reason, that we may become quiet, inoffensive, and peaceable christians ; nor yet, of any of its proper and legitimate operations upon divinely revealed truths. We only pretend to assert, what every one that pretends to reason must acknowledge ; namely, that there is a manifest distinction betwixt an express scripture declaration, and the conclusion or inference which may be deduced from it—and that the former may be clearly understood, even where the latter is but imperfectly, if at all perceived ; and that we are, at least, as certain of the declaration, as we can be of the conclusion, we draw from it— and that, after all, the conclusion ought not to be exalted above the premises, so as to make void the declaration for the sake of establishing our own conclusion—and that, therefore, the express commands to preserve and maintain inviolate christian unity and love ought not to be set aside to make way for exalting our inferences

D

above the express authority of God. Our inference upon the whole, is, that where a professing christian brother opposes or refuses nothing either in faith or practice, for which there can be expressly produced a "thus saith the Lord": that we ought not to reject him because he cannot see with our eyes as to matters of human inference—of private judgment. "Through thy knowledge shall the weak brother perish? How walketh thou not charitably? Thus we reason, thus we conclude, to make no conclusion of our own, nor of any other fallible fellow creature, a rule of faith or duty to our brother. Whether we refuse reason, then, or abuse it, in our so doing, let our brethren judge. But, after all, we have only ventured to suggest, what, in other words, the Apostle has expressly taught : namely, that the strong ought to bear with the infirmities of the weak, and not to please themselves. That we ought to receive him that is weak in the faith, because God has received him. In a word that we ought to receive one another, as Christ hath also received us to the glory of God. We dare not therefore, patronize the rejection of God's dear children, because they may not be able to see alike in matters of human inference—of private opinion ; and such we esteem all things, not expressly revealed and enjoined in the word of God. If otherwise, we know not what private opinion means. On the other hand, should our peaceful and affectionate overture for union and truth, prove offensive to any of our brethren ; or occasion disturbances in any of the churches ; the blame cannot be attached to us. We have only adventured to persuade, and if possible, to excite to the performance of an important duty, a duty equally incumbent upon us all. Neither have we pretended to dictate to *them*, what *they* should do. We have only proposed, what appeared to *us* most likely to promote the desired event ; humbly submitting the whole premises to their candid and impartial investigation ; to be altered, corrected, and amended, as they see cause ; or any other plan adopted that may appear more just and unexceptionable. As for ourselves, we have taken all due care, in the meantime to take no step, that might throw a stumbling block in the way ; that might prove now, or at any future period, a barrier to prevent the accomplishment of that most desirable object ; either by joining to support a party ; or by patronizing any thing as articles of faith or duty, not expressly revealed and enjoined in the divine standard ; as we are sure, whatever alterations may take place, *that* will stand. And that considerable alterations must and will take place in the standards of all the churches, before that glorious object can be accomplished, no man, that duly considers the matter, can possibly doubt. In so far then, we have at least, endeavoured to act consistently ; and with the same consistency would desire to be instrumental in erecting as many churches as possible, throughout the desolate places in God's heritage, upon the same catholic foundation ; being well persuaded, that every such erection will, not only in the issue, prove an accession to the general cause ; but will also, in the mean time, be a step towards it ; and of course,

will reap the first fruits of that blissful harvest, that will fill the
face of the world with fruit. For, if the first christian churches
walking in the fear of the Lord, in holy unity and unanimity, en-
joyed the comforts of the Holy Ghost, and were increased and edi-
fied; we have reason to believe, that walking in their footsteps will
every where, and at all times, ensure the same blessed privileges.
And it is in an exact conformity to their recorded and approved example, that we through grace, would be desirous to promote the
erection of churches : and this we believe to be quite practicable, if
the legible and authentic records of *their* faith and practice be han-
ded down to *us* upon the page of New Testament scripture : but
if otherwise, we cannot help it—Yet even in this case, might we not
humbly presume, that the Lord would take the will for the deed ;
for if there be first a willing mind, we are told, it is accepted, according to what a man hath, and not according to what he hath not.
It would appear, then, that sincerely and humbly adopting this model
with an entire reliance upon promised grace, we cannot, we shall
not, be disappointed. By this at least, we shall get rid of two great
evils, which we fear, are at this day, grievously provoking the Lord
to plead a controversy with the churches ; we mean the taking, and
giving of unjust offences ; judging and rejecting each other, in
matters wherein the Lord hath nor judged ; in a flat contradiction to
his expressly revealed will. But according to the principle adopted,
we can neither take offence at our brother for his private opinions,
if he be content to hold them as such ; nor yet offend him with
ours, if he do not usurp the place of the lawgiver ; and even suppose
he should, in this case we judge him, not for his *opinions*, but for his
presumption. "There is one lawgiver, who is able to save, and to
destroy : who art thou that judgest another?" But farther, to prevent mistakes, we beg leave, to explain our meaning in a sentence
or two, which might possibly be misunderstood. In page first, we say,
that no man has a right to judge his brother ; except in so far as he
manifestly violates the express letter of the law. By the law here,
and elsewhere, when taken in this latitude, we mean that whole revelation of faith and duty, expressly declared in the divine word,
taken together, or in its due connexion, upon every article : and
not any detached sentence. We understand it as extending to all
prohibitions, as well as to all requirements. "Add thou not unto
his words, lest he reprove thee, and thou be found a liar." We dare
therefore neither do, nor receive any thing, as of divine obligation,
for which there cannot be expressly produced a "thus saith the
Lord" either in express terms, or by approved precedent. According
to this rule we judge, and beyond it we dare not go. Taking this sentiment in connexion with the last clause of the fifth resolution ; we
are to be understood, of all matters of faith and practice, of primary and universal obligation ; that is to say, of express revelation :
that nothing be inculcated as such, for which there cannot be expressly produced a "thus saith the Lord" as above ; without, at
the same time, interfering directly or indirectly, with the private

judgment of any individual, which does not expressly contradict the express letter of the law, or add to the number of its institutions. Every sincere and upright christian, will understand and do the will of God, in every instance, to the best of his skill and judgment ; but in the application of the general rule to particular cases, there may, and doubtless will, be some variety of opinion and practice. This we see was actually the case in the apostolic churches, without any breach of christian unity. And if this was the case, at the erection of the christian church from amongst Jews and Gentiles, may we not reasonably expect, that it will be the same at her restoration, from under her long antichristian and sectarian desolations? With a direct reference to this state of things ; and, as we humbly think, in a perfect consistency with the foregoing explanations, have we expressed ourselves in page 10th ; wherein we declare ourselves ready to relinquish, whatever we have hitherto received as matter of faith or practice, not expressly taught and enjoined in the word of God ; so that we, and our brethren, might, by this mutual condescension, return together to the original constitutional unity of the christian church ; and dwell together in peace and charity. By this proposed relinquishment, we are to be understood, in the first instance, of our manner of holding those things, and not simply of the things themselves : for no man can relinquish his opinions or practices, till once convinced that they are wrong ; and this he may not be immediately, even supposing they were so. One thing however, he may do, when not bound by an express command, he need not impose them upon others, by any wise requiring their approbation ; and when this is done, the things, to them, are as good as dead ; yea, as good as buried too ; being thus removed out of the way. Has not the Apostle set us a noble example of this, in his pious and charitable zeal for the comfort and edification of his brother, in declaring himself ready to forego his rights (not indeed to break commandments) rather than stumble, or offend, his brother? And who knows not, that the Hebrew christians abstained from certain meats, observed certain days—kept the passover, circumcised their children, &c, &c.—while no such things were practised by the Gentile converts :—and yet no breach of unity, while they charitably forbore one with the other. But had the Jews been expressly prohibited, or the Gentiles expressly enjoined, by the authority of Jesus, to observe these things ; could they, in such a case, have lawfully exercised this forbearance? But where no express law is, there can be no formal, no intentional transgression ; although its implicit and necessary consequences had forbid the thing, had they been discovered. Upon the whole, we see one thing is evident ; the Lord will bear with the weaknesses, the involuntary ignorances, and mistakes of his people ; though not with their presumption. Ought they not, therefore, to bear with each other—"to preserve the unity of the spirit in the bond of peace ; forbearing one with another in love"—What saith the scripture? We say, then, the declaration referred to, is to be thus understood, in the first instance ; though we do not say, but something farther is intended. For certainly we may lawfully suspend both declaration and practice upon any subject, where the law is silent : when to do otherwise must prevent the accomplishment of an expressly commanded, and highly important duty : and such, confessedly, is the thing in question. What saith the Apostle? "All things are lawful for me : but all things are not expedient. All things are lawful for me ; but all things edify not." It seems, then, that amongst lawful things, which might be forborne ; that is, as we humbly conceive, things not expressly commanded ; the governing principle of the Apostle's conduct was the edification of his brethren of the church of God. A divine principle this, indeed! May the Lord God infuse it into all his people. Were all those nonpreceptive opinions and practises, which have been maintained and exalted to the destruction of the church's unity, counterbalanced with the breach of the express law of Christ, and the black catalogue of mischiefs which have necessarily ensued ; on which side, think you, would be the preponderance? When weighed in the balance with this monstrous complex evil, would they not all appear lighter than vanity? Who then would not relinquish a cent to obtain a kingdom! And here let it be noted, that it is not the renunciation of an opinion or practice as sinful, that is proposed or intended ; but merely a cessation from the publishing or preaching of it, so as to give offence ; a thing men are in the habits of doing every day for their private comfort, or secular emolument ; where the advantage is of infinitely less importance. Neither is there here any clashing of duties, as if to forbear was a sin, and also to practise was a sin ; the thing to be forborne being a matter of private opinion, which, though not expressly forbidden, yet are we, by no means, expressly commanded to practise,—Whereas we are expressly commanded to endeavor to maintain the unity of the spirit in the bond of peace. And what saith the Apostle to the point in hand? "Hast thou faith, saith he, have it to thyself before God. Happy is the man, that condemneth not himself, in the thing which he alloweth."

It may be farther added, that a still higher and more perfect degree of uniformity is intended, though neither in the first nor second instance, which are but so many steps toward it ; namely, the utter abolition of those minor differences, which have been greatly increased, as well as continued, by our unhappy manner of treating them ; in making them the subject of perpetual strife and contention. Many of the opinions which are now dividing the church, had they been let alone, would have been, long since, dead and gone ; but the constant insisting upon them, as articles of faith and terms of salvation, have so beat them into the minds of men, that, in many instances, they would as soon deny the Bible itself, as give up with one of those opinions. Having thus embraced contentions, and preferred divisions to that constitutional unity, peace and charity, so essential to christianity : it would appear, that the Lord, in righteous judgment, has abandoned his professing people to the awful scourge of those evils ; as in an instance somewhat similar, he formerly did his highly favored Israel. "My people, saith he, would not hearken to my voice. So I gave them up to their own hearts lusts, and they walked in their own counsels." "Israel hath made many altars to sin : therefore altars shall be unto him to sin." Thus, then, are we to be consistently understood, as fully and fairly intending, on *our* part, what we have declared and proposed to our brethren, as, to *our* apprehension, incumbent upon *them* and *us*, for putting an end forever, to our sad and lamentable schisms. Should any object and say, that after all, the fullest compliance with every thing proposed and intended, would not restore the church to the desired unity, as there might still remain differences of opinion and practice. Let such but duly consider, what properly belongs to the unity of the church, and we are persuaded, this objection will vanish. Does not the visible scriptural unity of the christian church consist in the unity of her public profession and practice ; and, under this, in the manfiest charity of her members, one toward another ; and not in the unity of the private opinion and practice of every individual? Was not this evidently the case in the Apostles' days, as has been already observed? If so the objection falls to the ground. And here, let it be noted, (if the hint be at all necessary,) that we are speaking of the unity of the church considered as a great visible professing body, consisting of many co-ordinate associations ; each of these, in its aggregate or associate capacity, walking by the same rule, professing and practising the same things. That this visible scriptural unity be preserved, without corruption, or breach of charity throughout the whole ; and in every particular worshipping society, or church ; is the grand desideratum—the thing strictly enjoined and greatly to be desired. An agreement in the expressly revealed will of God, is the adequate and firm foundation of this unity ; ardent prayer, accompanied with prudent peaceable, and persevering exertion, in the use of all scriptural means for accomplishing it, are the things humbly suggested, and earnestly recommended to our brethren. If we have mistaken the way, their charity will put us right : but if otherwise, their fidelity to Christ and his cause will excite them to come forth speedily, to assist with us in his blessed work.

After all, should any impeach us with the vague charge of Latitudinarianism (let none be startled at this gigantic term) it will prove as feeble an opponent to the glorious cause in which we, however weak and unworthy, are professedly engaged, as the Zamzummins did of old, to prevent the children of Lot from taking possession of their inheritance. If we take no greater latitude than the divine law allows, either in judging of persons or doctrines—either in profession, or practice (and this is the very thing we humbly propose and sincerely intend) may we not reasonably hope, that such a latitude will appear to every upright christian, perfectly innocent and unexceptionable? If this be Latitudinarianism, it must be a good thing—and therefore the more we have of it the better ; and may be it is, for we are told "the commandment is exceeding broad;" and we intend to go just as far as it will suffer us, but not one hair's breadth farther—so, at least, says our profession. And surely it will be time enough to condemn our practice, when it appears manifestly inconsistent with the profession, we have thus precisely and explicitly made. We here refer to the whole of the foregoing premises. But were this word as bad as it is long : were it stuffed with evil from beginning to end; may be, it better belongs to those, that brandish it so unmercifully at their neighbors; especially if they take a greater latitude than their neighbours do; or than the divine law allows. Let the case, then, be fairly submitted to all that know their Bible—to all that take upon them to see with their own eyes—to judge for themselves. And here let it be observed once for all, that it is only to such we direct our attention in the foregoing pages. As for those that either cannot, or will not see and judge for themselves, they must be content to follow their leaders, till they come to their eyesight; or determine to make use of the faculties, and means of information, which God has given them : with such, in the mean time, it would be useless to reason; seeing that they either confessedly cannot see; or have completely resigned themselves to the conduct of their leaders; and are therefore determined to hearken to none but them. If there be none such, however, we are happily deceived : but if so we are not the only persons that are thus deceived; for this is the common fault objected by almost all the parties to each other, viz, that they either cannot, or will not see; and it would be hard to think, they were all mistaken : the fewer there be, however, of this description the better. To all those, then, that are disposed to see and think for themselves, to form their judgment by the divine word itself, and not by any human explication of it—humbly relying upon and looking for, the promised assistance of divine teaching; and not barely trusting to their own understanding.—To all such do we gladly commit our cause; being persuaded, that, at least they will give it a very serious and impartial consideration; as being truly desirous to know the truth. To you, then, we appeal in the present instance, as we have also done from the beginning. Say, we beseech you, to whom does the charge of Latitudinarianism when taken in a bad sense (for we have supposed it may be taken in a good sense) most truly and properly belong. Whether to those that will neither add nor diminish any thing, as to matter of faith and duty; either to or from, what is expressly revealed and enjoined in the holy scriptures : or to those who pretend to go farther than this; or to set aside some of its express declarations and injunctions to make way for their own opinions, inferences, and conclusions? Whether to those who profess their willingness to hold communion with their acknowledged christian brethren, when they neither manifestly oppose nor contradict any thing expressly revealed and enjoined in the sacred standard : or to those who reject such, when professing to believe and practise whatever is expressly revealed and enjoined therein; without, at the same time being *alledged*, much less *found* guilty, of anything to the contrary: but instead of this, asserting and declaring their hearty assent and consent to every thing, for which there can be experssly produced a "thus saith the Lord," either in express terms, or by approved precedent. To which of these, think *ye*, does the odious charge of Latitudanarianism belong? Which of them takes the greatest latitude? Whether those that expressly judge and condemn where they have no express warrant for so doing; or those that absolutely refuse so to do? And we can assure our brethren, that such things are, and have been done, to our own certain knowledge; and even where we least expected it: and that it is to this discovery, as much as to many other things, that we stand indebted for that thorough conviction of the evil state of things in the churches, which has given rise to our association. As for our part, we dare no longer give our assent to such proceedings; we dare no longer concur in expressly asserting, or declaring, any thing in the name of the Lord, that he has not expressly declared in his holy word. And until such time as christians come to see the evil of doing otherwise, we see no rational ground to hope, that there can be either unity, peace, purity or prosperity, in the church of God. Convinced of the truth of this, we would humbly desire to be instrumental in pointing out to our fellow christians the evils of such conduct. And, if we might venture to give our opinion of such proceedings, we would not hesitate to say, that they appear to include three great evils—evils truly great in themselves, and at the same time productive of most evil consequences.

First, to determine expressly, in the name of the Lord, when the Lord has not expressly determined, appears to us a very great evil: see Deut. xviii—20. "The prophet that shall presume to speak a word in my name, which I have not commanded him to speak—even that prophet shall die." The Apostle Paul, no doubt, well aware of this, cautiously distinguishes betwixt his own judgment and the express injunctions of the Lord; See 1st Cor. 7, 25 and 40. Though at the same time, it appears that he was as well convinced of the truth and propriety of his declarations, and of the concurrence of the holy spirit with his judgment, as any of our modern determiners may be; for "I think saith he that I have the spirit of God:" and we doubt much, if the best of them would honestly say more than this: yet we see, that with all this, he would not bind the church with his conclusions; and for this very reason, as he expressly tells us, because, as to the matter on hand, he had no commandment of the Lord. He spoke by permission and not by commandment, as one that had obtained mercy to be faithful—and therefore would not forge his master's name by affixing it to his own conclusions; saying, "The Lord saith, when the Lord had not spoken."

A second evil is, not only judging our brother to be absolutely wrong, because he differs from our opinions; but, more especially, our judging him to be a transgressor of the law in so doing: and of course treating him as such, by censuring, or otherwise exposing him to contempt ; or, at least, preferring ourselves before him in our own judgment ; saying, as it were, stand by, I am holier than thou.

A third and still more dreadful evil is, when we not only, in this kind of way, judge and set at nought our brother ; but, moreover proceed as a church, acting and judging in the name of Christ ; not only to determine that our brother is wrong, because he differs from our determinations : but also in connexion with this, proceed so far as to determine the merits of the cause by rejecting him, or casting him out of the church, as unworthy of a place in her communion ;—and thus, as far as in our power, cutting him off from the kingdom of heaven. In proceeding thus, we not only declare, that, in our judgment, our brother is in an error ; which we may sometimes do in a perfect consistency with charity : but we also take upon us to judge, as acting in the name and by the authority of Christ, that his error cuts him off from salvation ; that continuing such he has no inheritance in the kingdom of Christ and of God. If not, what means our refusing him—or casting him out of the church, which is the kingdom of God in this world? For certainly if a person have no right, according to the Divine Word, to a place in the church of God upon earth, (which we say, he has not, by thus rejecting him) he can have none to a place in the church in heaven—unless we should suppose, that those whom Christ by his word rejects here, he will nevertheless receive hereafter. And surely it is by the word that every church pretends to judge ; and it is by this rule, in the case before us, that the person in the judgment of the church stands rejected. Now is not this to all intents and purposes determining the merits of the cause? Do we not conclude that the person's error cuts him off from all ordinary possibility of salvation, by thus cutting him off from a place in the church, out of which there is no ordinary possibility of salvation? Does he not henceforth become to us as a heathen man and a publican? Is he not reckoned amongst the number of those that are without, whom God judgeth? If not, what means such a solemn determination? Is it any thing, or is it nothing, for a person to stand rejected by the church of God? If such rejection confessedly leave the man still in the same safe and hopeful state, as to his spiritual interests ; then indeed, it becomes a matter of mere indifference ; for as to his civil and natural privileges, it interferes not with them. But the scripture gives us a very different view of the matter ; for there we see, that those that stand justly rejected by the church on earth, have no room to hope for a place in the church in heaven. "What ye bind on earth shall be bound in heaven" is the awful sanction of the churches judgment, in justly rejecting any person. Take away this, and it has no sanction at all. But the church rejecting, always pretends to have acted justly in so doing ; and if so, whereabouts does it confessedly leave the person rejected, if not in a state of damna-

E

tion; that is to say, if it acknowledge itself to be a church of Christ, and to have acted justly. If after all, any particular church acting thus, should refuse the foregoing conclusion, by saying, we meant no such thing concerning the person rejected—we only judged him unworthy of a place amongst *us;* and therefore put him away; but there are other churches that may receive him. We would be almost tempted to ask such a church, if those other churches be churches of Christ; and if so, pray what does it account itself? Is it anything more or better than a church of Christ? And, whether if those other churches do their duty, as faithful churches, any of them would receive the person it had rejected? If it be answered, that, in acting faithfully, none of those other churches either could, or would receive him; then, confessedly, in the judgment of this particular church, the person ought to be universally rejected: but, if otherwise, it condemns itself of having acted unfaithfully, nay, cruelly towards a christian brother, a child of God; in thus rejecting him from the heritage of the Lord; in thus cutting him off from his father's house as the unnatural brethren did the beloved Joseph. But even suppose some one or other of those unfaithful churches should receive the outcast, would their unfaithfulness in so doing nullify, in the judgment of this more faithful church, its just and faithful decision in rejecting him? If not, then, confessedly, in its judgment, the person still remains under the influence of its righteous sentence, debarred from the kingdom of heaven; that is to say, if it believe the scriptures, that what it has righteously done upon earth, is ratified in heaven. We see no way, that a church acting *thus,* can possibly get rid of this *awful conclusion;* except it acknowledges that the person it has rejected from its communion, still has a right to the communion of the church; but if it acknowledge *this*—whereabouts does it leave itself, in thus shutting out a fellow-christian, an acknowledged brother, a child of God!! Do we find any parallel for such conduct in the inspired records, except in the case of Diotrephes, of whom the Apostle says, "who loveth to have the pre-eminence among them, receiveth us not—prating against us with malicious words, and not content therewith, neither doth he himself receive the brethren, and forbiddeth them that would, and casteth them out of the church."

But farther, suppose another church should receive this castaway, this person, which this faithful church supposed itself to have righteously rejected: would not, the church so doing, incur the displeasure, nay, even the *censure,* of the church that had rejected him? and, we should think justly too, if he deserved to be rejected. And would not this naturally produce a schism betwixt the churches? Or, if it be supposed that a schism did already exist, would not this manifestly tend to perpetuate and increase it? If one church receiving those, whom another puts away, will not be productive of schism, we must confess, we cannot tell what would. That church, therefore must surely act very schismatically—very unlike a church of Christ, which necessarily pre-supposes, or produces schism, in order to shield an oppressed fellow-christian, from the dreadful consequences of its unrighteous proceedings. And is not this confessedly the case with every church, which rejects a person from its communion, while it acknowledges him to be a fellow-christian ; and in order to excuse this piece of cruelty, says, he may find refuge some place else ; some other church may receive him? For as we have already observed, if no schism did already exist, one church receiving those whom another has rejected, must certainly make one. The same evils also will as justly attach to the conduct of an individual, who refuses, or breaks communion with a church, because it will not receive, or make room for, his private opinions, or self-devised practices, in its public profession and managements—for, does he not, in this case, actually take upon him to judge the church, which he thus rejects, as unworthy of the communion of christians? And is not this to all intents and purposes declaring it, in his judgment, excommunicate ; or at least worthy of excommunication?

Thus have we briefly endeavored to shew our brethren, what evidently appears to us to be the heinous nature and dreadful consequences of that truly latitudinarian principle and practice, which is the bitter root of almost all our divisions, namely, the imposing of our private opinions upon each other, as articles of faith or duty ; introducing them into the public profession and practice of the church, and acting upon them, as if they were the express law of Christ, by judging and rejecting our brethren that differ with us in those things ; or, at least, by *so* retaining them in our public profession and practice, that our brethren cannot join with us, or we with them, without becoming actually partakers of those things, which they, or we, cannot, in conscience approve ; and which the word of God no where expressly enjoins upon us. To cease from all such things, by simply returning to the original standard of christianity—the profession and practice of the primitive church, as expressly exhibited upon the sacred page of New Testament scripture, is the only possible way, that we can perceive, to get rid of those evils. And we humbly think that a uniform agreement in *that* for the preservation of charity would be infinitely preferable to our contention and divisions : nay, that such a uniformity is the very thing that the Lord requires, if the New Testament be a perfect model—a sufficient formula for the worship, discipline and government of the christian church. Let *us* do, as we are there expressly told *they* did, say as *they* said : that is, profess and practise as therein expressly enjoined by precept and precedent, in every possible instance, after *their* approved example ; and in so doing we shall realize, and exhibit, all that unity and uniformity, that the primitive church possessed, or that the law of Christ requires. But if after all, our brethren can point out a better way to regain and preserve that christian unity and charity expressly enjoined upon the church of God, we shall thank them for the discovery and cheerfully embrace it.

Should it still be urged, that this would open a wide door to latitudinarianism, seeing all that profess christianity, profess to receive the holy scriptures; and yet differ so widely in their religious sentiments. We say, let them profess what they will, their difference in religious profession and practice originates in their departure from what is expressly revealed and enjoined; and not in their strict and faithful conformity to it— which is the thing we humbly advise for putting an end to those differences. But you may say, do they not already all agree in the letter, though differing so far in sentiment? However this may be, have they all agreed to make the letter their rule; or rather to make it the subject matter of their profession and practice? Surely no; or else they would all profess and practice the same thing. Is it not as evident as the shining light, that the scriptures exhibit but one and the self same subject matter of profession and practice; at all times, and in all places;—and, that therefore, to say as it declares, and to do as it prescribes, in all its holy precepts, its approved and imitable examples, would unite the christian church in a holy sameness of profession and practice, throughout the whole world? By the christian church throughout the world, we mean the aggregate of such professors, as we have described in props. 1 and 8th, page 7th; even all that mutually acknowledge each other as christians, upon the manifest evidence of their faith, holiness, and charity. It is such only we intend, when we urge the necessity of christian unity. Had only such been all along recognized, as the genuine subjects of our holy religion, there would not, in all probability, have been so much apparent need for human formulas, to preserve an external formality of professional unity, and sound-ness in the faith: but artificial and superficious characters need artificial means to train and unite them. A manifest attachment to our Lord Jesus Christ in faith, holiness, and charity, was the origi-nal criterion of christian character—the distinguishing badge of our holy profession—the foundation and cement of christian unity. But now, alas! and long since, an external name—a mere educa-tional formality of sameness in the profession of a certain standard, or formula of human fabric, with a very moderate degree of, what is called, morality; forms the bond and foundation—the root and reason, of ecclesiastical unity. Take away from such the technia of their profession—the shiboleth of party; and what have they more? What have they left to distinguish, and hold them together? As for the Bible, they are but little beholden to it; they have learned little from it; they know little about it; and therefore de-pend as little upon it. Nay, they will even tell you, it would be of no use to them without their formula; they could not know a Papist from a Protestant by *it;* that merely by *it,* they could neither keep themselves nor the church right for a single week; you might preach to them what you please; they could not distinguish truth from error. Poor people! it is no wonder they are so fond of their formula. Therefore they that exercise authority upon them, and tell them what they are to believe, and what they are to do, are called benefactors. These are the reverend, and right reverend authors, upon whom they *can*, and *do*, place a more entire and implicit confidence, than upon the holy Apostles and Prophets; those plain, honest, unassuming men, who would never venture to say, or do, any thing, in the name of the Lord, without an express revelation from heaven; and, therefore, were never distinguished by the venerable titles of rabbi, or reverend; but just simply Paul, John, Thomas, &c. *These* were but servants. They did not assume to legislate; and therefore neither assumed, nor received, any honorary titles amongst men : but merely such as were descriptive of their office. And how, we beseech you, shall this gross and prevalent corruption be purged out of the visible professing church, but by a radical reform; but by returning to the original simplicity, the primitive purity, of the christian institution and, of course, taking up things just as we find them upon the sacred page. And, who is there, that knows any thing of the present state of the church, who does not perceive, that it is greatly overrun with the aforesaid evils? Or, who that reads his Bible, and receives the impressions, it must necessarily produce upon the receptive mind, by the statements it exhibits; does not perceive, that such a state of things is as distinct from genuine christianity, as oil is from water?

On the other hand, is it not equally as evident, that not one of all the erroneous tenets, and corrupt practices, which have so defamed and corrupted the public profession and practice of christianity, could ever have appeared in the world, had men kept close by the express letter of the divine law—had they thus held fast that form of sound words contained in the holy scriptures, and considered it their duty so to do :—unless they blame those errors and corruptions upon the very form and expression of the scriptures; and say, that, taken in their letter and connexion, they immediately, and at first sight, as it were, exhibit the picture they have drawn. Should any be so bold as to assert this, let them produce their performance, the original is at hand; and let them shew us line for line; expression for expression; precept and precedent for practice; without the torture of criticism, inference, or conjecture; and then we shall honestly blame the whole upon the Bible; and thank those that will give us an expurged edition of it; call it constitution, or formula, or what you please; that will not be liable to lead the simple unlettered world into those gross mistakes, those contentions, schisms, excommunications and persecutions, which have proved so detrimental and scandalous to our holy religion.

Should it be farther objected, that even this strict literal uniformity would neither infer, nor secure unity of sentiment.—It is granted, that, in a certain degree, it would not; nor, indeed, is there any thing, either in scripture, or the nature of things, that should induce us to expect an entire unity of sentiment, in the present imperfect state. The church may, and we believe will, come to such a scriptural unity of faith and practice, that there will be no schism in the body; no self-preferring sect of professed and acknowledged christians, rejecting and excluding their brethren. *This* cannot be, however, till the offensive and excluding causes be removed; and every one knows what *these* are. But that all the members should have the same identical views of all divinely revealed truths; or that there should be no difference of opinion among them, appears to us morally impossible, all things considered. Nor can we conceive, what desirable purpose such a unity of sentiment would serve: except to render useless some of those gracious, self-denying, and compassionate precepts of mutual sympathy and forbearance, which the word of God enjoins upon his people. Such, then, is the imperfection of our present state— Would to God it might prove, as it ought, a just and humbling counterbalance to our pride! Then, indeed, we would judge one another no more about such matters. We would rather be conscientiously cautious to give no offense; to put no stumbling block, or occasion to fall in our brother's way. We would then no longer exalt our own opinions and inferences to an equality with express revelation, by condemning and rejecting our brother, for differing with us in those things.

But although it be granted, that the uniformity we plead for, would not secure unity of sentiment; yet we should suppose, that it would be as efficacious for that purpose, as any human expedient, or substitute whatsoever. And here we would ask, have all, or any, of those human complications been able to prevent divisions, to heal breaches, or to produce and maintain unity of sentiment, even amongst those who have most firmly, and solemnly, embraced them? We appeal for this to the history of all the churches, and to the present divided state of the church at large. What good then have those divisive expedients accomplished, either to the parties that have adopted them, or to the church universal; which might not have been as well secured, by holding fast in profession and practice that form of sound words, contained in the divine standard; without at the same time, being liable to any of those dangerous and destructive consequences, which have necessarily ensued upon the present mode? Or will any venture to say, that the scriptures thus kept in their proper place, would not have been amply sufficient, under the promised influence of the divine spirit to have produced all that unity of sentiment, which is necessary to a life of faith and holiness; and also to have preserved the faith and worship of the church as pure from mixture and error, as the Lord intended; or as the present imperfect state of his people can possibly admit? We should tremble to think that any christian should say, that they would not. And if to use them thus, would be sufficient for those purposes; why resort to other expedients—to expedients, which, from the beginning to this day, have proved utterly insufficient; nay, to expedients, which have always produced the very contrary effects, as experience testifies. Let none here imagine that we set any certain limits to the Divine intention, or to the greatness of his power when we thus speak, as if a certain degree of purity from mixture and error were not designed for the church in this world, or attainable by his people upon earth ; except in so far as respects the attainment of an angelic or unerring perfection ; much less, that we mean to suggest, that a very moderate degree of unity and purity should content us. We only take it for granted, that such a state of perfection is neither intended, nor attainable in this world, as will free the church from all those weaknesses, mistakes, and mismanagements, from which she will be completely exempt in heaven :—however sound and upright she may now be in her profession, intention, and practice. Neither let any imagine, that we here, or elsewhere suppose, or intend to assert, that human standards, are intentionally set up in competition with the Bible ; much less in opposition to it. We fairly understand and consider them as human expedients, or as certain doctrinal declarations. of the sense in which the compilers understood the scriptures ; designed, and embraced, for the purpose of promoting and securing, that desirable unity and purity, which the Bible alone, without those helps, would be insufficient to maintain and secure. If this be not the sense of those that receive and hold them, for the aforesaid purpose, we should be glad to know what it is. It is, however, in this very sense that we take them up, when we complain of them, as not only unsuccessful, but also as unhappy expedients ; producing the very contrary effects. And even suppose it were doubtful, whether or not those helps have produced divisions ; one thing at least is certain, that they have not been able to prevent them ; and now that divisions do exist, it is as certain, that they have no fitness nor tendency to heal them ; but the very contrary, as fact and experience clearly demonstrate. What shall we do then to heal our divisions? We must certainly take some other way than the present practice, if they ever be healed ; for it expressly says, they must, and shall, be perpetuated forever. Let all the enemies of christianity say amen. But let all christians, continually say, forbid it, O Lord. May the good Lord subdue the corruptions, and heal the divisions of his people. Amen and amen.

After all that has been said, some of our timid brethren may possibly still object, and say ; we fear, that without the intervention of some definite creed or formula, you will justly incur the censure of latitudinarianism ; for how, otherwise, detect and exclude Arians, Socinians, &c. &c? To such we would reply, that if to profess, inculcate, and practice, neither more nor less, neither any thing else nor otherwise, than the Divine Word expressly declares respecting the entire subject of faith and duty ; and simply to rest in *that*, as the expression of our faith, and rule of our practice ; will not amount to the profession, and practical exhibition, of Arianism Socinianism, &c. &c. but merely to one and the self same thing, whatever it may be called ; then is the *ground* that we have taken, the *principle* that we advocate, in nowise chargeable with latitudinarianism. Should it be still farther objected that all these sects, and many more, profess to receive the Bible, to believe it to be the word of God; and therefore will readily profess to believe and practise whatever is revealed and enjoined therein; and yet each will understand it his own way, and of course practise accordingly : nevertheless, according to the plan proposed, you receive them all. We would ask, then, do all these profess, and practise, neither more, nor less, than what we read in the Bible—than what is expressly revealed and enjoined therein? If so they all profess and practise the same thing; for the Bible exhibits but one and the self-same thing to all. Or, is it their own inferences and opinions that they, in reality, profess and practise? If so, then upon the ground that we have taken, they stand rejected, as condemned of themselves; for thus professing one thing, when in fact and reality they manifestly practise another. But perhaps you will say, that although a uniformity in profession, and it may be in practice too, might thus be produced; yet still it would amount to no more than merely a uniformity in words, and in the external formalities of practice; while the persons thus professing and practising, might each entertain his own sentiments, how different soever these might be. Our reply is, if so, they could hurt no body but himself; besides, if persons thus united, professed and practised all the same things, pray, who could tell, that they entertained different sentiments; or even in justice suppose it, unless they gave some evident intimation of it? which, if they did, would justly expose them to censure; or to rejection, if they repented not; seeing the offence, in this case, must amount to nothing less than an express violation of the expressly revealed will of God—to a manifest transgression of the express letter of the law; for we have declared, that except in such a case, no man, in our judgment, has a right to judge, that is, to condemn, or reject, his professing brother.— Here, we presume, there is no greater latitude assumed, or allowed, on either side, than the law expressly determines, But we would humbly ask, if a professed agreement in the terms of any standard be not liable to the very same objection? If, for instance, Arians, Socinians, Arminians, Calvinists, Antinomians, &c. &c. might not all subscribe the Westminster Confession, the Athenasian Creed, or the doctrinal articles of the Church of England. If this be denied, we appeal to historical facts; and, in the mean time, venture to assert, that such things are, and have been done. Or will any say, that a person might not with equal ease, honesty, and consistency, be an Arian, or a Socinian, in his heart, while subscribing the Westminster Confession, or the Athenasian Creed, as while making his unqualified profession to believe every thing that the scriptures declare concerning Christ? to put all that confidence in him; and to ascribe all that glory, honor, thanksgiving, and praise to him, professed, and ascribed to him in the Divine Word? If you say not it follows of undeniable consequence, that the wisdom of men, in those compilations, has effected, what the Divine Wisdom either could not, would not, or did not do, in that

all-perfect and glorious revelation of his will, contained in the holy
Scriptures. Happy emendation! Blessed expedient! Happy indeed, for the church, that Athenasius arose in the fourth century,
to perfect what the holy apostles and prophets had left in such a rude
and unfinished state. But if, after all, the Divine Wisdom did not
think proper to do any thing more, or any thing else, than is already
done in the Sacred Oracles, to settle and determine those important
points ; who can say that he determined such a thing should be done
afterwards? Or has he any where given us any intimation of such
an intention?

Let it here be carefully observed that the question before us is
about human standards designed to be subscribed, or otherwise
solemnly acknowledged, for the preservation of ecclesiastical unity
and purity ; and therefore of course, by no means, applies to the
many excellent performances, for the scriptural elucidation and
defence of divinely revealed truths, and other instructive purposes.
These, we hope, according to their respective merit, we as highly
esteem, and as thankfully receive, as our brethren. But farther,
with respect to unity of sentiment, even suppose it ever so desirable, it appears highly questionable, whether such a thing can at all
be secured, by any expedient whatsoever ; especially if we consider, that it necessarily pre-supposes in so far, a unity or sameness
of understanding. Or, will any say, that, from the youth of seven-
teen to the man of four score—from the illiterate peasant, up to the
learned prelate ; all the legitimate members of the church entertain the same sentiments under their respective formulas. If not,
it is still but a mere verbal agreement, a mere shew of unity. They
say an amen to the same forms of speech, or of sound words, as
they are called ; without having, at the same time, the same views
of the subject ; or, it may be, without any determinate views of it
at all. And what is still worse, this profession is palmed upon the
world, as well as upon the too credulous professors themselves, for
unity of sentiment ; for soundness in the faith : when in a thousand
instances, they have, properly speaking, no faith at all : that is to
say, if faith necessarily pre-supposes a true and satisfactory conviction of the scriptural evidence and certainty of the truth of the
propositions we profess to believe. A cheap and easy orthodoxy
this, to which we may attain by committing to memory a catechism ;
or professing our approbation of a formula, made ready to our
hand ; which we may or may not have once read over ; or even if
we have, yet may not have been able to read it so correctly and
intelligently, as to clearly understand one single paragraph from
beginning to end ; much less to compare it with, to search and try
it by, the holy Scriptures ; to see if these things be so. A cheap
and easy orthodoxy this, indeed, to which a person may thus attain,
without so much as turning over a single leaf of his Bible ; whereas
Christ knew no other way of leading us to the knowledge of himself, at least has prescribed no other, but by searching the Scriptures, with reliance upon his holy Spirit. A person may, however,

F

by this short and easy method, become as orthodox as the Apostle
Paul (if such superfical professions, such mere hearsay verbal
repetitions can be called orthodoxy) without ever once consulting
the Bible ; or so much as putting up a single petition for the Holy
Spirit to guide him into all truth ; to open his understanding to
know the Scriptures ; for, his form of sound words truly believed,
if it happened to be right, must, without more ado, infallibly secure
his orthodoxy. Thrice happy expedient! But is there no latitudinarianism in all this? Is not this taking a latitude, in devising
ways and means for accomplishing divine and saving purposes,
which the Divine law has no where prescribed ; for which the
Scriptures no where afford us, either precept or precedent? Unless
it can be shewn, that making human standards to determine the
doctrine, worship, discipline, and government, of the church, for
the purpose of preserving her unity and purity ; and requiring an
approbation of them as a term of communion ; is a Scripture institution. .Far be it from us, in the mean time, to alledge, that the
church should not make every spiritual exertion, in her power,
to preserve her unity and purity ; to teach and train up her members in the knowledge of all divinely revealed truth ; or to say, that
the evils, above complained of, attached to all that are in the habits of
using the aforesaid helps ; or that this wretched state of things,
however general, necessarily proceeds from the legitimate use of
such ; but rather, and entirely, from the abuse of them ; which is
the very and only thing, that we are all along opposing, when we
allude to those subordinate standards.—(An appellation this, bye the
bye, which appears to us highly paradoxical, if not utterly inconsistent, and full of confusion.)

But however this may be, we are by no means to be understood
as at all wishing to deprive our fellow-christians of any necessary
and possible assistance to understand the scriptures : or to come to
a distinct and particular knowledge of every truth they contain ;—
for which purpose the Westminister Confession and Catechisms,
may with many other excellent performances, prove eminently
useful. But, having served ourselves of these, let our profiting
appear to all, by our manifest acquaintance with the Bible ; by
making our profession of faith and obedience, by declaring its divine dictates, in which we acquiesce as the subject matter and rule
of both—in our ability to take the Scripture in its connexion upon
these subjects, so as to understand one part of it by the assistance
of another—and in manifesting our self knowledge, our knowledge
of the way of salvation, and of the mystery of the christian life, in
the express light of divine revelation ; by a direct and immediate
reference to, and correct repetition of, what it declares upon these
subjects—We take it for granted, that no man either knows God,
or himself, or the way of salvation, but in so far, as he has heard
and understood his voice upon those subjects, as addressed to him
in the Scriptures ; and that, therefore, whatever he has heard and
learned of a saving nature, is contained in the express terms of the

Bible. If so, in the express terms, in and by which, "he hath heard and learned of the Father," let him declare it. This by no means forbids him to use helps : but, we humbly presume, will effectually prevent him from resting either in them or upon them ; which is the evil so justly complained of—from taking up with the directory instead of the object to which it directs. Thus will the whole subject of his faith and duty, in so far as he hath attained, be express-ly declared, in a "thus saith the Lord." And, is it not worthy of remark, that, of whatever use other books may be, to direct and lead us to the Bible ; or to prepare and assist us to understand it ; yet the Bible never directs us to any book but itself. When we come forward then as christians to be received by the church, which, properly speaking, has but one book. "For to it were committed the oracles of God ;" let us hear none else. Is it not upon the credible profession of our faith in, and obedience to, its divine contents, that the church is bound to receive applicants for admis-sion? And does not a profession of our faith and obedience, neces-sarily pre-suppose a knowledge of the dictates we profess to believe and obey? Surely, then, we can declare them ; and as surely, if our faith and obedience be divine, as to the subject matter, rule, and reason of them, it must be a "thus saith the Lord ;" if otherwise, they are merely human ; being taught by the precepts of men. In the case then before us, that is, examination for church member-ship, let the question no longer be what does any human system say of the primitive or present state of man ; of the person, offices and relations of Christ, &c. &c. or of this, that, or the other duty ; but what says the Bible? Were this mode of procedure adopted, how much better acquainted with their Bibles would christians be? What an important alteration would it also make in the education of youth? Would it not lay all candidates for admission into the church under the happy necessity of becoming particularly acquainted with the holy Scriptures? whereas, according to the present practice, thousands know little about them.

One thing still remains that may appear matter of difficulty or objection to some ; namely, that such a close adherence to the express letter of the Divine word, as we seem to propose, for the restoration and maintenance of christian unity ; would not only interfere with the free communication of our sentiments one to another, upon religious subjects ; but must, of course, also neces-sarily interfere with the public preaching and expounding of the Scriptures, for the edification of the church. Such as feel disposed to make this objection, should justly consider that one of a similar nature, and quite as plausible, might be made to the adoption of human standards ; especially when made as some of them confess-edly are, "the standard for all matters of doctrine, worship, disci-pline, and government." In such a case it might, with as much justice, at least, be objected to the adopters ; you have now no more use for the Bible ; you have got another book which you have adopted as a standard for all religious purposes—you have no farther use for explaining the Scriptures, either as to matter of faith or duty : for this you have confessedly done already in your standard, wherein you have determined all matters of this nature. You also profess to hold fast the form of sound words, which you have thus adopted ; and therefore you must never open your mouth upon any subject in any other terms than those of your standard. In the mean time, would any of the parties, which has thus adopted its respective standard, consider any of these charges just? If not, let them do as they would be done by. We must confess, however, that for our part, we cannot see how, with any shadow of consistency, some of them could clear themselves, especially of the first ; that is to say, if words have any determinate meaning ; for certainly it would appear almost, if not altogether, incontrovertible ; that a book adopted by any party as its standard for all matters of doctrine, worship, discipline, and government ; must be considered as the Bible of that party. And after all that can be said in favor of such a performance, be it called Bible, standard, or what it may ; it is neither any thing more nor better, than the judgment, or opinion of the party composing or adopting it ; and therefore wants the sanction of a Divine authority ; except in the opinion of the party which has thus adopted it. But can the opinion of any party, be it ever so respectable, give the stamp of a Divine authority to its judgments? If not, then every human standard is deficient in this leading, all-important, and indispensable property of a rule, or standard, for the doctrine, worship, discipline, and government of the church of God. But without insisting farther upon the intrinsic and irremediable deficiency of human standards, for the above purpose, (which is undeniably evident, if it be granted that a Divine authority is indispensably necessary to constitute a standard, or rule for divine things : such as is the constitution, and managements ; the faith, and worship of the christian church)—we would humbly ask would any of the parties consider as just, the foregoing objections, however conclusive and well founded, all or any of them may appear? We believe they would not. And may we not with equal consistency hold fast the expressly revealed will of God, in the very terms in which it is expressed in his Holy Word, as the very expression of our faith, and express rule of our duty ; and yet take the same liberty that they do, notwithstanding their professed and steadfast adherence to their respective standards? We find they do not cease to expound, because they have already expounded, as before alledged; nor yet do they always confine themselves to the express terms of their respective standards ; yet they acknowledge them to be their standards, and profess to hold them fast. Yea, moreover, some of them profess, and, if we may conclude from facts, we believe each of them is disposed to defend, by occasional vindications (or testimonies, as some call them,) the sentiments they have adopted, and engrossed in their standards ; without, at the same time, requiring an approbation of those occasional performances, as a term of communion. And what should hinder us, or any, adopting the Divine Standard, as aforesaid, with equal consistency to do the same; for the vindication of the divine truths expressly revealed and enjoined therein? To say that we cannot believe and profess the truth; understand one another; inculcate and vindicate the faith and law of Christ; or do the duties incumbent upon christians, or a christian church, without a human standard; is not only saying, that such a standard is quite essential to the very being of christianity, and of course must have existed before a church was, or could be formed: but it is also saying, that without such a standard, the Bible would be quite inadequate, as a rule of faith and duty; or rather, of no use at all; except to furnish materials for such a work—whereas the church of Ephesus, long before we have any account of the existence of such a standard, is not only mentioned, with many others, as in a state of existence; and of high attainments too; but is also commended for her vigilance and fidelity, in detecting and rejecting false apostles. "Thou hast tried them which say they are apostles, and are not, and hast found them liars." But should any pretend to say, that although such performances be not essential to the very being of the church, yet are they highly conducive to its well being and perfection. For the confutation of such an assertion, we would again appeal to church history, and existing facts, and leave the judicious and intelligent christian to determine.

If after all that has been said, any should still pretend to affirm, that the plan we profess to adopt and recommend, is truly latitudinarian, in the worst and fullest sense of the term; inasmuch as it goes to make void all human efforts to maintain the unity and purity of the church, by substituting a vague and indefinite approbation of the Scriptures as an alternative for creeds, confessions, and testimonies; and thereby opens a wide door for the reception of all sorts of characters and opinions into the church. Were we not convinced by experience, that notwithstanding all that has been said, such objections would likely be made; or that some weak persons might possibly consider them as good as demonstration; especially when proceeding from highly influential characters (and there have not been wanting such in all ages to oppose, under various plausible pretences, the unity and peace of the church) were it not for these considerations, we should content ourselves with what we have already advanced upon the whole of the subject, as being well assured, *that* duly attended to, there would not be the least room for such an objection: but to prevent if possible such unfounded conclusions; or if this cannot be done, to caution and assist the too credulous and unwary professor, that he may not be carried away all at once with the high-toned confidence of bold assertion;—we would refer him to the overture for union in truth contained in the foregoing address. Union in truth, amongst all the manifest subjects of grace and truth, is what we advocate. We carry our views of union no farther than *this;* nor de we presume to recommend it upon any other principle than truth alone.

Now surely truth is something certain and definite; if not, who will take upon him to define and determine it? This we suppose God has sufficiently done already in his Holy Word. That men therefore truly receive and make the proper use of the Divine word for walking together in truth and peace, in holiness and charity, is, no doubt, the ardent desire of all the genuine subjects of our holy religion. This we see, however, they have not done, to the awful detriment, and manifest subversion of, what we might almost call, the primary intention of christianity. We dare not therefore follow their example, nor adopt their ruinous expedients. But does it therefore follow, that christians may not, or cannot, take proper steps to ascertain that desirable and preceptive unity, which the Divine word requires, and enjoins? Surely no—at least we have supposed no such thing ;—but on the contrary, have overtured to our brethren, what appears to us undeniably just, and scripturally evident ; and which we humbly think, if adopted and acted upon, would have the desired effect—adopted and acted upon, not indeed as a standard for the doctrine, worship, discipline, and government of the church ; for it pretends not to determine these matters ; but rather supposes the existence of a fixed and certain standard of divine original ; in which every thing that the wisdom of God saw meet to reveal and determine, for *these*, and all other purposes, is expressly defined and determined ; betwixt the christian and which, no medium of human determination ought to be interposed. In all this, there is surely nothing like the denial of any lawful effort, to promote and maintain the churches' unity ; though there be a refusal of the unwarrantable interposition, of an unauthorized and assuming power.

Let none imagine, that we are here determining upon the merits of the overture, to which, in the case before us, we find it necessary to appeal, in our own defence, against the injustice of the supposed charge above specified. To the judgment of our brethren have we referred that matter ; and with them we leave it. All we intend, therefore, is to avail ourselves so far, of what we have done, as to shew, that we have no intention whatsoever of substituting a vague indefinite approbation of the Scriptures, as an alternative for creeds, confessions, and testimonies ; for the purpose of restoring the church to her original constitutional unity and purity. In avoiding Sylla we would cautiously guard against being wrecked upon the Charybdis. Extremes we are told are dangerous. We therefore suppose a middle way ; a safe way ; so plainly marked out by unerring wisdom, that, if duly attended to under the Divine direction, the wayfaring men, though fools, need not err therein ; and of such is the kingdom of God ; "for he hath chosen the foolish things of the world to confound the things that are wise." We therefore conclude, it must be a plain way, a way most graciously and most judiciously adapted to the capacity of the subjects ; and consequently not the way of subscribing, or otherwise approving human standards, as a term of admission into his church ; as a test and defence of orthodoxy; which even the compilers themselves are not always agreed about; and which nineteen out of twenty of the Lord's people cannot thoroughly understand. It must be a way very far remote from logical subtilties, and metaphysical speculations; and as such we have taken it up, upon the plainest and most obvious principles of divine revelation, and common sense—the common sense, we mean of christians, exercised upon the plainest and most obvious truths and facts, divinely recorded for their instruction. Hence we have supposed in the first place, the true discrimination of christian character to consist in an intelligent profession of our faith in Christ and obedience to him in all things according to the Scriptures; the reality of which profession is manifested by the holy consistency of the tempers and conduct of the professors, with the express dictates, and approved examples of the Divine word. Hence we have humility, faith, piety, temperance, justice, charity, &c. professed and manifested in the first instance by the persons' professing with self-application the convincing, humbling, encouraging, pious, temperate, just and charitable doctrines and precepts of the inspired volume, as exhibited and enforced in its holy and approved examples; and the sincerity of this profession evidently manifested, by the consistency of the professor's temper and conduct with the entire subject of his profession; either by an irreproveable conformity like good Zachariah and Elizabeth, which is of all things most desirable; or otherwise, in case of any visible failure, by an apparently sincere repentance, and evident reformation. Such professors, and such only, have we supposed to be, by common consent, truly worthy the christian name. Ask from the one end of heaven to the other, the whole number of such intelligent and consistent professors as we intend, and have described, and we humbly presume, there will not be found one dissenting voice. They will all acknowledge with one consent, that the true discrimination of christian character consists in these things; and that the radical, or manifest want, of any of the aforesaid properties, completely destroys the character.

We have only here taken for granted, what we suppose no rational professor will venture to deny; namely, that the Divine Word contains an ample sufficiency upon every of the foregoing topics to stamp the above character; if so be, that the impressions which its express declarations are obviously calculated to produce, be truly received; for instance, suppose a person profess to believe, with application to himself, that whole description of human depravity and wretchedness which the Scriptures exhibit of fallen man, in the express declarations and dismal examples of human wickedness therein recorded; contrasted with the holy nature. the righteous requirements, and inflexible justice of an infinitely holy, just, and jealous God; would not the subject matter of such a profession be amply sufficient to impress the believing mind with the most profound humility, self-abhorrence, and dreadful apprehension of the tremendous effects of sin? Again should the person profess to believe, in connexion with this, all that the Scriptures declare of the sovereign love, mercy, and condescension of God, towards guilty, depraved, rebellious man, as the same is manifested in Christ, and in all the gracious declarations, invitations and promises, that are made in and through him, for the relief and encouragement of the guilty, &c. would not all this, taken together, be sufficient to impress the believing mind with the most lively confidence, gratitude, and love? Should this person, moreover, profess that delight and confidence in the Divine Redeemer—that voluntary submission to him—that worship and adoration of him, which the Scriptures expressly declare to have been the habits and practice of his people; would not the subject matter of this profession be amply sufficient to impress the believing mind with that dutiful disposition, with that gracious veneration, and supreme reverence, which the word of God requires? And should not all this taken together satisfy the church, in so far, in point of profession? If not, there is no alternative but a new revelation; seeing that to deny this, is to assert, that a distinct perception, and sincere profession, of whatever the word declares upon every point of faith and duty, is not only insufficient, as a doctrinal means, to produce a just and suitable impression in the minds of the believing subject; but is also insufficient to satisfy the church, as to a just and adequate profession :—if otherwise, then it will necessarily follow, that not every sort of character, but that one sort only, is admissible upon the principle we have adopted; and, that by the universal consent of all, that we, at least, dare venture to call christians, *this* is acknowledged to be, exclusively, the true christian character. Here then we have a fixed point, a certain description of character, which combines in every professing subject, the scriptural profession, the evident manifestation, of humility, faith, piety, temperance, justice, and charity; instructed by, and evidently answering to, the entire declaration of the Word, upon each of those topics : which, as so many properties, serve to constitute the character. Here, we say, we have a fixed and at the same time sweeping distinction; which, as of old, manifestly divides the whole world, however, other ways distinguished, into but two classes only. "We know," said the Apostle, evidently speaking of such, "that we are of God, and the whole world lieth in wickedness."

Should it be enquired concerning the persons included in this description of character, whether they be Arminians, or Calvinists, or both promiscuously huddled together? It may be justly replied, that, according to what we have proposed, they can be nominally neither, and of course not both; for we call no man master on earth; for one is our master, even Christ and all we are brethren— are christians by profession; and, as such, abstract speculation and argumentative theory make no part, either of our profession, or practice. Such professors, then, as we intend, and have described, are just what their profession and practice make them to be; and this we hope has been scripturally, and, we might add, satisfactorily

defined ; in so far, at least, as the limits of so brief a performance
would admit. We also entertain the pleasing confidence, that the
plan of procedure which we have ventured to suggest, if duly
attended to, if fully reduced to practice, would necessarily secure
to the professing subject all the advantages of divinely revealed
truth, without any liability to conceal, or diminish, or to misrepre-
sent it ; as it goes immediately to ascribe every thing to God respecting his sovereignty, independence, power, wisdom, goodness,
justice, truth, holiness, mercy, condescension, love and grace, &c.
which is ascribed to him in his word ; as also to receive whatever
it declares concerning the absolute dependence of the poor, guilty,
depraved, polluted creature, upon the Divine will, power, and grace,
for every saving purpose : a just perception and correspondent profession of which, according to the Scriptures, is supposed to constitute that fundamental ingredient in christian character, true
evangelical humility. And so of the rest. Having thus, we hope,
scripturally and evidently determined the character with the proper
mode of ascertaining it, to the satisfaction of all concerned : we
next proceed to affirm with the same scriptural evidence, that
amongst such, however situated, whether in the same or similar
associations, there ought to be no schisms, no uncharitable divisions ;
but that they ought all mutually to receive, and acknowledge each
other as brethren. As to the truth of this assertion, they are all
likewise agreed without one dissenting voice. We next suggest
that for this purpose they ought to all walk by the same rule, to
mind and speak the same thing, &c. and that this rule is, and ought
to be, the Divine Standard. Here again we presume there can be
no objection, no, not a single dissenting voice. As to the rule
itself, we have ventured to alledge that the New Testament is the
proper and immediate rule, directory, and · formula, for the New
Testament church, and for the particular duties of christians ; as
the Old Testament was for the Old Testament church, and for the
particular duties of the subject under that dispensation ; at the
same time by no means excluding the old as fundamental to, illus-
trative of, and inseparably connected with, the new ; and as being
every way of equal authority, as well as of an entire sameness with
it, in every point of moral natural duty ; though not immediately
our rule, without the intervention and coincidence of the new ; in
which our Lord has taught his people, by the ministry of his holy
Apostles, all things whatsoever thay should observe and do, till the
end of the world. Thus we come to the one rule, taking the Old
Testament as explained and perfected by the new, and the new as
illustrated and enforced by the old ; assuming the latter as the proper and immediate directory for the christian church, as also for
the positive and particular duties of christians, as to all things
whatsoever they should observe and do. Farther, that in the observance of this Divine rule—this authentic and infallible directory,
all such may come to the desirable coincidence of holy unity and
uniformity of profession and practice ; we have overtured that they

all speak, profess, and practice, the very same things, that are exhibited upon the sacred page of New Testament Scripture, as spoken and done by the Divine appointment and approbation ; and that this be extended to every possible instance of uniformity, without addition or diminution ; without introducing any thing of private opinion, or doubtful disputation, into the public profession or practice of the church. Thus and thus, have we overtured to all intents and purposes, as may be clearly seen by consulting the overture itself ; in which, however, should any thing appear not sufficiently explicit, we flatter ourselves it may be fully understood, by taking into consideration what has been variously suggested, upon this important subject, throughout the whole of these premises ; so that if any due degree of attention be paid, we should think it next to impossible, that we could be so far misunderstood, as to be charged with Latitudinarianism in any usual sense of the word. Here we have proposed but one description of character as eligible, or indeed as at all admissible to the rights and privileges of christianity. This description of character we have defined by certain and distinguishing properties, which not only serve to distinguish it from every other ; but in which all the real subjects themselves are agreed, without one exception : all such being mutually and reciprocally acknowledged by each other, as legitimate members of the church of God. All these moreover agreeing in the indispensable obligation of their unity ; and in the one rule by which it is instructed—and also in the preceptive necessity of an entire uniformity in their public profession and managements for promoting and preserving this unity—that there should be no schism in the body ; but that all the members should have the same care one for another—yet in many instances unhappily, and, we may truly say, involuntarily differing through mistake and mismanagement ; which it is our humble desire and endeavour to detect and remove, by obviating every thing that causeth difference ; being persauded that as truth is one and indivisible wherever it exists ; so all the genuine subjects of it, if disentangled from artificial impediments, must and will necessarily fall in together, be all on one side, united in one profession, acknowledge each other as brethren, and love as children of the same family. For this purpose we have overtured a certain and determinate application of the rule, to which we presume there can be no reasonable objection, and which, if adopted and acted upon, must, we think, infallibly produce the desired effect, unless we should suppose that to say and do, what is expressly said and done before our eyes upon the sacred page, would offend the believer ; or that a strict uniformity, and entire scriptural sameness in profession and practice, would produce divisions and offences amongst those, who are already united in one spirit, one Lord, one faith, one baptism, one hope of their calling, and in one God and father of all, who is above all, and through all, and in them all ; as is confessedly the case with all of this character throughout all the churches. To induce to this we have also attempted to call their attention to the heinous nature and awful consequences of schism, and to that evil anti-scriptural principle from which it necessarily proceeds. We have likewise endeavored to shew, we humbly think with demonstrable evidence, that there is no alternative, but either to adopt that scriptural uniformity we have recommended, or else continue as we are, bewildered in schisms, and overwhelmed with the accursed evils inseparable from such a state. It remains now with our brethren to determine upon the whole of these premises; to adopt, or to reject, as they see cause; but, in the mean time, let none impeach us with the latitudinarian expedient of substituting a vague indefinite approbation of the Holy Scriptures, as an alternative for the present practice of making the approbation of human standards a term of communion; as it is undeniably evident that nothing can be farther from our intention. Were we to judge of what we humbly propose and urge as indispensably necessary for the reformation and unity of the church, we should rather apprehend, that there was reason to fear a charge of a very different nature; namely, that we aimed at too much strictness, both as to the description of character which we say ought only to be admitted, and also as to the use and application of the rule. But should this be the case, we shall cheerfully bear with it; as being fully satisfied, that not only the common sentiment of all apparently sincere, intelligent and practical christians is on our side; but that also the plainest and most ample testimonies of the inspired volume sufficiently attest the truth and propriety of what we plead for, as essential to the scriptural unity and purity of the christian church; and this we humbly presume is what we should incessantly aim at. It would be strange, indeed, if in contending earnestly for the faith, once delivered to the saints, we should overlook those fruits of righteousness—that manifest humility, piety, temperance, justice and charity—without which faith itself is dead being alone. We trust we have not so learned Christ: if so be, we have been taught by him, as the truth is in Jesus, we must have learned a very different lesson indeed. While we would therefore insist upon an entire conformity to the Scriptures in profession, that we might all believe and speak the same things, and thus be perfectly joined together in the same mind and in the same judgment; we would, with equaly scrupulosity, insist upon and look for, an entire conformity to them in practice, in all those whom we acknowledge as our brethren in Christ. "By their fruits ye shall know them." "Not every one that saith unto me, Lord, Lord, shall enter into the kingdom of heaven: but he that doeth the will of my father which is in heaven. Therefore whosoever heareth those sayings of mine, and doeth them not, shall be likened unto a foolish man which built his house upon the sand. Woe unto you scribes and pharisees, hypocrites, for ye say and do not." We therefore conclude, that to advocate unity alone, however desirable in itself without at the same time purging the church of apparently unsanctified characters—even of all that cannot shew their faith by their works, would be, at best, but a poor, superficial, skin-deep reformation. It is from such characters, then, as the proposed reformation, if carried into effect, would entirely deprive of a name and a place in the church, that we have the greatest reason to apprehend a determined and obstinate opposition. And alas! there are very many of this description ; and in many places, of considerable influence—But neither should this discourage us, when we consider the expressly revealed will of God upon this point, Ezek. 44 6—9, with Matt. 13, 15—17, I. Cor. 5, 6— 13, with many other Scriptures. Nor, in the end, will the multitude of unsanctified professors, which the proposed reformation would necessarily exclude, have any reason to rejoice in the unfaithfulness of those, that either through ignorance, or for filthy lucre sake, indulged them with a name and place in the church of God. These unfaithful stewards—these now mistaken friends, will one day be considered by such as their most cruel and treacherous enemies. These, then, are our sentiments, upon the entire subject of church reformation ; call it latitudinarianism, or puritanism, or what you please : and *this* is the reformation for which we plead. Thus, upon the whole, have we briefly attempted to point out those evils, and to prevent those mistakes, which we earnestly desire to see obviated for the general peace, welfare, and prosperity of the church of God. Our dear brethren, giving credit to our sincere and well meant intentions, will charitably excuse the imperfections of our humble performance ; and by the assistance of their better judgment correct those mistakes, and supply those deficiencies, which in a first attempt of this nature may have escaped our notice. We are sorry, in the mean time, to have felt a necessity of approaching so near, the borders of controversy, by briefly attempting to answer objections which we plainly foresaw would, through mistake or prejudice, be made against our proceedings ; controversy making no part of our intended plan. But such objections and surmises having already reached our ears from different quarters, we thought it necessary to attend to them ; that, by so doing, we might not only prevent mistakes, but also save our friends the trouble of entering into verbal disputes in order to remove them ; and thus prevent, as much as possible, that most unhappy of all practices sanctioned by the plausible pretence of zeal for the truth ;— religious controversy amongst professors. We would therefore humbly advise our friends to concur with us in our professed and sincere intention to avoid this evil practice. Let it suffice to put into the hands of such as desire information what we hereby publish for that purpose. If this, however, should not satisfy, let them give in their objections in writing : we shall thankfully receive, and seriously consider, with all due attention, whatever comes before us in this way ; but verbal controversy we absolutely refuse. Let none imagine, that by so saying, we mean to dissuade christians from affording all the assistance they can to each other, as humble enquirers after the truth. To decline this friendly office would be to refuse the performance of an important duty. But certainly there is a manifest difference between speaking the truth in love for the edification of our brethren ; and attacking each other with a spirit of controversial hostility, to confute and prove each other wrong. We believe it is rare to find one instance of this kind of arguing, that does not terminate in bitterness. Let us therefore cautiously avoid it. Our Lord says, Math. 18, 7, woe unto the world because of offences Scott in his incomparable work lately published in this country, called his Family Bible, observes in his notes upon this place, 'that our Lord here intends all these evils within the 'church, which prejudice men's minds against his religion or any 'doctrine of it. The scandalous lives, horrible oppressions, cru-'elties, and iniquities of men called christians ; their divisions and 'bloody contentions ; their idolatries and superstitions, are, at this 'day, the *great offences* and *causes of stumbling*, to Jews, Mahome-'tans, and Pagans, in all the four quarters of the globe ; and they 'furnish infidels of every discription, with their most dangerous 'weapons against the truth. The acrimonious controversies, agi-'tated amongst those who agree in the principal doctrines of the 'gospel, and their mutual contempt and reviling of each other, 'together with the extravagant notions and wicked practices found 'among them, form the grand prejudice in the minds of multitudes 'against evangelical religion ; and harden the hearts of hereticks, 'pharisees, disguised infidels, and careless sinners, against the 'truths of the gospel. In these and numberless other ways, it may 'be said, "woe be to the world because of offences;" for the devil, 'the sower of these tares, makes use of them in deceiving the na-'tions of the earth, and in murdering the souls of men. In the 'present state of human nature it must needs be, that such offences 'should intervene ; and God has wise and righteous reasons for 'permitting them ; yet we should consider it as the greatest of 'evils, to be accessary to the destruction of souls ; and an awful 'woe is denounced against every one, whose delusions or crimes 'thus stumble men, and set them against the only method of salva-'tion.'' We conclude with an extract from the Boston Anthology, which, with too many of the same kind that might be adduced, furnish a mournful comment upon the text—we mean, upon the sorrowful subject of our woeful divisions and corruptions. The following reply to the Rev. Mr. Cram, missionary from Massachusetts to the Senecas, was made by the principal chiefs and warriors of the six nations in council assembled at Buffaloe creek, state of New-York, in the presence of the agent of the United States for Indian affairs, in the summer of 1805. 'I am come, brethren,' said the missionary, 'to enlighten your minds, and to instruct you how to 'worship the Great Spirit, agreeably to his will ; and to preach to 'you the gospel of his son Jesus Christ. There is but one way to 'serve God, and if you do not embrace the right way you cannot be 'happy hereafter.' To which they reply, 'Brother we understand 'that your religion is written in a book. You say that there is but

'one way to worship and serve the Great Spirit. If there be but
'one religion, why do you white people differ so much about it?
'Why not all agree as you can all read the book? Brother, we do
'not understand these things. We are told your religion was given
'to your forefathers; we also have a religion which was given to
'our forefathers. It teaches us to be *thankful* for all the favors we
'receive—to *love* one another, and to be *united*. We never quarrel
'about religion. We are told you have been preaching to the white
'people in this place. Those people are our neighbors; we are
'acquainted with them. We will wait a little to see what effect
'your preaching has upon *them*. If we find it does them good,
'makes them *honest*, and *less* disposed to cheat Indians; we will
'then consider again of what you have said.' Thus closed the
conference! Alas! poor people! how do our divisions and corruptions stand in your way? What a pity that you find us not upon
original ground, such as the Apostles left the primitive churches?
Had we but exhibited to you their unity and charity; their humble,
honest, and affectionate deportment towards each other and towards
all men: you would not have had those evil and shameful things
to object to our holy religion, and to prejudice your minds against
it. But your conversion, it seems, awaits our reformation—awaits
our return to primitive unity and love. To this may the God of
mercy speedily restore us, both for your sakes and our own; that
his way may be known upon earth, and his saving health among all
nations. Let the people praise thee, O God; let all the people
praise thee. Amen and amen.

POSTSCRIPT.

THE publication of the foregoing address has been delayed much
longer than was at first expected, through an unforeseen difficulty
of obtaining paper of the quality intended. This difficulty and de-
tention has also interfered with the publication of the discourse
delivered at the first general meeting of the society, held in Washington, November 2d, in pursuance of the 7th resolution; (see
page 4th) which discourse the committee has requested Mr. Campbell to have published, as soon as conveniency may serve for that
purpose. At the first monthly meeting of the committee, Decem-
ber 14, (see resolution 6th, page 4,) the following considerations
and proposals for the better carrying into effect the highly interest-
ing and comprehensive object of the foregoing address, were submitted and received with approbation, viz. That considering the
very extensive and important design for which we have associated,
as specified in the foregoing pages; wherein we propose and urge

the necessity of a thorough reformation in all things civil and religious according to the word of God, as a duty of indispensable obligation upon all the highly favored subjects of the gospel; and especially in this country, where the Lord has been graciously pleased to favor his professing people with such ample opportunities, for the prosecution and accomplishment of those blessed and desirable purposes; it behoves us, in so doing, to exert our utmost energies, in every possible direction that may conduce to render successful, this arduous and important undertaking.

Besides what has been already agreed upon, and recommended in the foregoing pages, there yet remains two things of apparently great importance for promoting the grand object of our association; which this committee would do well to consider, as they seem to fall within the prescribed limits of its operation; and also as it appears to be within the compass of its power to take effectual steps for ascertaining the advantages, which the things intended, if duly executed, would appear obviously calculated to produce. The first of these is a catechetical exhibition of the fulness and precision of the holy scriptures upon the entire subject of christianity—an exhibition of that complete system of faith and duty expressly contained in the sacred oracles; respecting the doctrine, worship, discipline, and government of the christian church. The second thing intended is a periodical publication, for the express purpose of detecting and exposing the various anti-christian enormities, innovations and corruptions, which infect the christian church; which counteract and oppose the benign and gracious tendency of the gospel—the promotion and establishment of the Redeemer's kingdom upon earth; by means of which an infinitely good and gracious God has designed to bless the nations—to ameliorate as much as possible the present wretched and suffering state of mankind; upon the success and establishment of which depends the spiritual and temporal welfare of every individual of the human family. Whatever therefore has a tendency to undermine, or in anywise to counteract and oppose the interest of this benign and gracious institution of infinite goodness and mercy, becomes an evil of no small magnitude, how trifling soever it might otherwise appear. "Take us the foxes, the little foxes that spoil our vines; for our vines have tender grapes." Cant 2, 15. Such a publication from the nature and design of it, might with propriety be denominated The Christtian Monitor.

The former of these, namely, a catechetical exhibition of the fulness and precision of the sacred scriptures upon the entire subject of faith and duty would, if duly executed, demonstrably evince their perfect sufficiency independent of human inference—of the dictates of private judgment; and would, at the same time, inevitably lead the professing subject to learn every thing, respecting his faith and duty, at the mouth of God, without any reference to human authority—to the judgment or opinions of men. This would, at once, free the great majority of professing christians from that perplexing uncertainty and implicit faith to which so many of them are unhappily subjected, by the interposition of human definitions and opinions between them and the Bible ; many of which are erroneous ; and also many of which they are unable to understand, so as to determine certainly, whether they be just and scriptural, or not. By such an exhibition, therefore, would professed christians be delivered, not only from these perplexing and dangerous evils ("their faith," by this means, "no longer standing in the wisdom of men, but in the power of God ; not in the words which man's wisdom teacheth, but which the Holy Ghost teacheth,") but they would also become better acquainted with the scriptures of truth—with that all-important word which shall judge them in the last day :—and at the same time, would come to possess a much more ample and enlarged view of the alone sufficiency and perfection of the scriptures themselves ; advantages these of no small moment to the interest of christianity. A performance of this nature might with apparent propriety, be called the Christian Catechism.

In consequence of these considerations it is proposed and intended, with the approbation and under the patronage of the Christian Association of Washington, to forward as fast as possible the publication of the works above described, viz, To publish in numbers monthly by subscription, commencing with the year 1810—a work entitled the Christian Monitor, each number to consist of 24 pages, stitched in blue, price 12½ cents, type and paper as in the foregoing address. The numbers to be delivered to the subscribers at the respective places appointed for distribution. The execution of this work to commence as soon as 500 annual subscribers can be obtained. It is to be understood, that a number for each month will be duly delivered ; though it is probable that the first two or three numbers may come together, as it is not likely, that the number of subscribers above specified can be obtained in time to commence the publication in the month of January, now so near at hand.

Also to prepare for the press and proceed to publish as soon as a competent number of subscribers can be obtained, a work entitled the Christian Catechism, to consist of upwards of one hundred pages, type and paper as above, price 50 cents. There will be prefixed to this work a dissertation upon the perfection and sufficiency of the holy scriptures ; in which care will be taken to detect and expose, that unhappy ingenuity, which has been so frequently exerted to prevent and wrest them, from the obvious purpose for which they were graciously designed.

ERRATA—Page 2, line 5, the comma point should be after agreed, and not after upon.
Do line 7, for titled read designated.
Page 7, line 15, for spurious read specious.
Page 16, line 3, for grounds read ground.
Page 29, line 23, for preaching read practising.
Page 32, line 39, for would read could.

Breinigsville, PA USA
03 February 2011
254815BV00001B/6/P